How Online Gambling Is Destroying America

By Jack Alan Levine and John Rabe

BAD BET How Online Gambling Is Destroying America
By Jack Alan Levine and John Rabe
Published by Great Hope Publishing LLC, Windermere, Florida
Cover Design by Scott Wolf
www.JackAlanLevine.com
Email: Jack@JackAlanLevine.com
Copyright 2026 Jack Alan Levine and John Rabe. All rights reserved.

Neither the publisher nor the author is engaged in rendering advice or services to the individual reader. Neither the authors nor the publisher shall be liable or responsible for any loss, injury, or damage allegedly arising from any information or suggestion in this book. The opinions expressed in this book represent the personal views of the authors and not of the publisher and are for informational purposes only.

Many of the various stories of people in this book draw from real life experience, at certain points involving a composite of stories. In some instances, people's names have been changed in the stories to protect privacy.

ISBN NUMBER 978-0-9904097-9-3 (PAPERBACK)
ISBN NUMBER 978-1-7356075-2-8 (EPUB)

LIBRARY OF CONGRESS CONTROL NUMBER: 2026935955

FIRST EDIITON

This book is about America's destruction as caused by the gambling epidemic that has poisoned our country and is killing our youth.

DEDICATION

We dedicate this book to all those who struggled since the beginning of time with gambling addiction.

To those who have lost the battle and suffered the consequences of a gambling addiction, we grieve for you and your families who are so severely affected. And to those who have overcome it and have enjoyed the benefits of life without it, we rejoice with you.

We celebrate your courage, strength and victory. As we personally know the joy, happiness, peace and success you have enjoyed throughout your life, having discarded and defeated this disgusting, deadly addiction.

We dedicate this book to all people alive today and to their children and grandchildren and the generations of children to come, in the hopes it will warn, inspire and encourage them to run as far away from possible from this hideous and addictive disease which is coming for their souls, wallets, families and futures.

With love and hope,

Jack and John

Table of Contents

Dedication 5

Introduction 10

PART I
VIEW FROM THE FIELD

Chapter 1   The Problem 13

Chapter 2   A Firsthand View 17

Chapter 3   Jack Meet Gambling,
Gambling Meet Jack 21

Chapter 4   Growing Problem............................27

Chapter 5   It's My Father's Fault....................33

Chapter 6   How Much Pain Can You Take? 39

Chapter 7   Some Are Trying To Help 43

Chapter 8   Is Everyone Who Bets an Addict? 45

Chapter 9   If You Haven't Experienced It,
You Probably Can't Relate to It.......47

Chapter 10 The Poison Spreads 49

Chapter 11 The Beginning of the End 51

Chapter 12 They're Out to Get You! 55

Chapter 13 Suckers...57

Chapter 14 Wake Up America...
Before It's Too Late!..........................61

Chapter 15 You Can't Win.................................65

Chapter 16 The End Result 71

CHAPTER 17 WHAT SHOULD WE DO?
THE SOLUTION 73

CHAPTER 18 I DID MY OWN RESEARCH,
JUST LIKE SIGMUND FREUD 77

CHAPTER 19 MY RESEARCH PROVED MY THEORY 81

CHAPTER 20 WHAT HAPPENS NEXT? 83

PART II
VIEW FROM THE PRESS BOX

INTRODUCTION 88

CHAPTER 21 THE LEGALIZATION 91

CHAPTER 22 THE SPREAD OF APPS............................ 95

CHAPTER 23 THE COMPLICITY OF THE SPORTS LEAGUES 99

CHAPTER 24 THE EFFECT ON SPORTS 107

CHAPTER 25 THE EFFECT ON PEOPLE

1. An Epidemic in Gambling Addiction......... 121

2. Children Gambling...................................... 136

Signs of Gambling Addiction......................... 145

CHAPTER 26 SOLUTIONS... 149

CLOSING THOUGHTS... 152

SPECIAL THANKS 154

REFERENCES 156

PART I
VIEW FROM THE FIELD

Get the Down and Dirty, Firsthand Insight and Inside Scoop from Someone Who's Been There, Done It, Lived It, Been Crushed By It, and Survived!

BY: JACK ALAN LEVINE

Introduction

We wanted to write this book years ago when online poker became prevalent and we saw young high school and college students, as well as professionals (both men and women), housewives and retirees start to gamble feverishly and ferociously, virtually nonstop on their phones and computers.

The busyness of life held us back from writing at that time, but finally we could not stand it anymore or restrain ourselves any longer as the advent of online sports gambling has spread and accelerated to supercharged levels.

It's one thing to see a car going a few miles over the speed limit on your neighborhood street and think, 'hey that's not the safest thing in the world; somebody should tell them to slow down.' Yet it's another thing to see six cars going a hundred miles an hour down your street with an inch between them and pedestrians lined up on the side of the street. You know something bad is going to happen. There will be a crash as cars spin out of control and people are going to die.

That is the analogy we draw to where we are today with online gambling. People are going to get hurt badly and some will die. It's bad; it's very, very bad.

So, in this book we want to sound the alarm. We want this to be a wake-up call to our readers, their families, and their friends. We would like you to take action! Elect leaders who will restore our country to sanity at every level including our cities, counties and states. Men and woman who will not join with or tolerate professional sports selling their souls to the devil at the expense of our children, spouses, families, future hopes, dreams, and lives. You can do that at the ballot box. You can do that by writing letters to politicians. You can do it by boycotting professional sports leagues and teams that allow and endorse gambling advertising. You can do that by taking a stand in your local communities. You can also do that by letting other people know just how bad this problem is.

Now, it's years later since online poker arrived and we realize what Instagram, Facebook and TikTok, and Snapchat have done to our children and the negative impact their products have had on the lives of our children and families.

These platforms have opened up a gateway to hell for our children as predators come right through phones and computers into your children's faces. They are deviously able to bypass you and all of the protective shields you think you have put around your children to protect them. It has led and is leading our children down the road of pornography, sex addiction, loss of self-worth, anxiety, depression, and sometimes even suicide.

This is exactly what is happening here with the onslaught of online gambling and its expansion and explosion throughout our country.

It is more than bad news; it is a disaster. In five or ten years we will be bemoaning the woes of what has happened and see the effects on so many people who lost everything because of gambling, and the despair and destruction it has caused.

Let's get ahead of the curve. At very least, read this book and get the knowledge, information, and facts firsthand that can help you decide whether we are right or wrong in our perspective. There is a term gamblers use when they are certain that a bet cannot lose, that the bet is a sure thing. It's called 'a lock.'

Well, it's a *lock* that gambling will destroy the lives of many and that the onslaught of online gambling is the beginning of the end for America as we know it. Please read on. See the facts for yourself and make your own decision. Then please, act on it!

Chapter 1

THE PROBLEM

Tragically, gambling has become ingrained into our youth as an everyday part of their lives. Whether it's football, basketball, baseball, hockey, soccer, tennis, NASCAR, golf, college or pro, it doesn't matter. You could always bet on the outcome of a given sporting event, but now you can bet on it live as it happens. You can bet quarter by quarter, down by down, pitch by pitch, play-by-play, basket by basket, and the lines change constantly with every new play and every minute that goes by.

This is the equivalent of putting a heroin needle into the arms of our youth.

In the old days you had to go to the racetrack or go to Las Vegas to legally place a bet. You could be a winner over the course of an evening, or even a couple of days. But very few, if any, win consistently over time. Of course, many placed bets with illegal local (and then later online) bookmakers.

As we know, many paid a tragic price. Some with their lives, some with their families, some with their futures, as gambling addiction is a very, very real problem. It has destroyed many lives, hopes, dreams, individuals and families.

With the advent of the Internet exploding in our lives, we have 24/7 online access to many good things but also many horrible things, like 24/7 access to poker and to sports gambling. It is appalling. My heart breaks for the generation of young people and college students who thought they could become like poker star Chris Moneymaker, and others who dropped out of school, or gave up careers to pursue the lure of easy gambling winnings as poker players.

I would equate it to those who smoked cigarettes and died of cancer or are suffering from a smoking-related disease. It is a bad choice, but it is their choice whether to smoke or not and their choice whether to gamble or not. However, imagine if cigarette smoke was in your house every day and you had to inhale everywhere you went. That's how it is with gambling today.

Literally, gambling it is now part of the sport itself. With advertising today and the league now partnering with todays leading sports books like DraftKings, FanDuel and Hard Rock Bet to appeal to its viewers, they make people believe they are missing out if they do not have a bet on the game or the play or the quarter. They make people believe there is easy money to be made solely by using their amazing talent and knowledge of the game to outsmart the house. That is a joke and a huge lie! As we know, nobody outsmarts the house and over time the house always wins.

We have turned the nation of people who love their sports into a nation of gamblers who are overwhelmed and possessed by its lure of quick riches and easy money. It is no longer about the greatness of the game or the brilliance of the plays or the players, but about the outcome of the game verses the point spread, the halftime score, the over under total, the sinking of the basket, and the covering of the betting line. That is truly a tragedy!

Columnist Charles Gasparino (New York Post) commenting on the National Football League's Commissioner Roger Goodell wrote:

> The league has increased engagement through cynical ploys such as sports gambling. We all know how gambling destroys lives and drives people to financial ruin. Yet in partnership with betting apps and sport books, Goodell and Co. has supplied this opium to the masses, transforming what was once the simple pleasure of watching the game into an all-consuming, addictive experience. It's Vegas on your iPhone and it continues to lure men, especially

young men, hooked on a product that bombards
them with progressive tropes (similar messages).

Chapter 2

A FIRSTHAND VIEW

I personally know what it's like. I know what it's like to feel the excitement and the relief to know that my bet has been placed. I equate it to a drug addict taking a drug and getting excited knowing the effects are going to kick in.

I know what it's like to wait anxiously for the score or results of the game, and to watch the game and to live and die with every pitch, every basket, every catch, every touchdown.

So, I know what it's like to get addicted to sports gambling and have it take over every aspect of your life and, by that process, ruin your life. Believe me it stinks! If you don't believe me, ask anyone else whose life has been impacted by their gambling habit.

I could share hundreds, maybe thousands of more stories of what happened (specific bets, games and what I felt as I gambled on certain days and nights) when dealing with my gambling issues. In order to save you from reading the longest book in the world, I have narrowed it down to some highlighted examples and stories for this book. I think they will all make the point quite clearly. The same point! There were some highs, a lot more lows and it all added up to a devastating addiction.

Regarding my own addiction and struggles:

I remember being on the fast-track on Madison Avenue. I was a rising, young, hot-shot executive; I had everything going for me. But I also remember coming home at night and my head hitting the pillow; I would just think, 'My life stinks; is this all there is? I just go to work, I gamble, I use drugs, I party. Could this really be all there is to life?' I knew there had to be more.

I came to realize there was more but, I can tell you, in the throes of my addiction, even though I was functioning in the outside world and at my job, inside, I was destroyed. And I came to realize that this addiction had me in its grip like an animal caught in a trap. I realized I was over the line this time, I couldn't get back. It was one of the most harrowing feelings in my life, to just know that, truly, I was trapped in this addiction, and it had me and that was a devastating feeling.

And that's what most addicts feel. It's what addiction does to you on the inside; it's the destroying of your soul, of your emotions, your energy, your enthusiasm, of everything that you're trying to accomplish. The addiction takes control and you realize that it has you trapped. It is a dreadful feeling. It is like a prison or a trap, not one you can see physically but one you feel emotionally all the time.

Addiction also has a dramatic effect on the family, and not a good one. It breaks our hearts as we watch our loved one's struggle and spiral down into the pit of addiction. As well as being recovering addicts, my wife and I are parents of an addict, whose addiction we dealt with. It was horrifying to both watch and experience. So, I do know firsthand what it's like to be an addict myself and what's it's like to deal with a loved one's addiction.

My first introduction to gambling was when I was about 12 years old. My mom and dad took me on a trip to Florida where we went to Disney and some other places. I remember being in the hotel room and my father taught me how to play blackjack. We were playing for change (dimes, nickels, and quarters). I kicked dad's butt that day and wound up winning about thirteen dollars. He was not very happy about it. I had not seen my father unhappy often but, believe me, he was not very happy that day. It wasn't that it was a great deal of money to him, I think his pride was just insulted.

I think Dad wanted to teach me a lesson about gambling thinking I would lose to him and never gamble again. It backfired! But, for me, it was very exciting.

I saw that I could gamble and win, that if the cards went my way, it would be a good thing and it was exciting to play.

Chapter 3
JACK MEET GAMBLING, GAMBLING MEET JACK

And then my introduction to gambling really continued to extend. There was a bingo game every Wednesday night at Greystone Jewish Center, a temple in Yonkers, New York (where we lived). I'll never forget Ellen Siegel, one of the neighborhood ladies, who used to take me and a couple of my high school friends to bingo with her on Wednesday nights. We would be there with all the old ladies and I remember Hy the bingo caller, he was the guy from the temple who called out the numbers on the balls as they popped out of the machine.

There had to be a couple of hundred people there and we got multiple bingo cards. I loved the ink stampers we stamped the cards with when the ball called out matched a number on our card. We'd play and occasionally we won. One time I won $50! It felt like winning a million dollars and I couldn't wait to go to bingo every Wednesday with Ellen Siegel. The big jackpot was $250.00, and it was just phenomenal. I loved the thought of playing and loved the thought of winning. One night I won the big jackpot, at that time, one of the greatest nights of my life.

Then when I was 16, my father took me to the race-track, Yonkers Raceway, for the first time. I will never forget, I made a $2 bet that my dad made for me because you couldn't bet yourself unless you were 18. I bet on the number five horse; it was a photo finish between the number three horse and the number five horse. And this was standard-bred racing, often called harness racing, where the drivers sit behind the horse in a sulky, often referred to as a "race bike." It was a photo finish and we had to wait for the results to come in. The results finally came and the number three horse won. So, I actually lost the photo finish. But I'll never forget turning to my dad and saying, 'Let me get this right. You mean if I had bet the three instead of the five, I would have just won $16?' He said, 'Yeah.' I was hooked from that moment on. It was like sticking a heroin needle in my arm.

As the high school years went by, my friends and I would spend many a night at Yonkers Raceway, often parking a mile away and walking just to save the dollar parking fee. Because, at that point, we were going to the track with anywhere between $20 and $40. Back then, that was a big stash of money for the night. Even before I got started going to Yonkers Raceway, in high school, some friends and I started playing poker and acey deucey for money. There were about five of us in a rotating game, me and my friends Mark, Scott, Bob, Evan, and Kenny. We would play on Saturday mornings and afternoons, usually for three, four, or even five hours. You could make some money, maybe come away with 20 to 60 bucks at the end of the day, which was big money for us at the time.

So, we had these card games going on, we had bingo when we were kids, and later in high school we had the track. Ahh the track! I'm not going to say it wasn't fun and exciting. Getting to yell at the horses and the drivers and handicapping the races thinking how smart we were, betting on and watching the races. It was exhilarating, exciting and fun, at least in the beginning. And sometimes we won. But the more we won, the more we bet. Well, the more we lost, the more we bet, too. That is only part of the insanity of gambling.

I remember one time in particular, I was there with this older kid from the neighborhood, Stu, great guy; he was a great baseball player in his younger days and we were on the same neighborhood softball team the *DeHaven Demolishers*. Stu had a bit of a drug problem, but I really liked him; he took a liking to me, as well, and we both loved to go to the track. Matter of fact, when I got my first new car, a 1976 Chevrolet Monte Carlo, we broke it in by driving an hour and a half from Yonkers to Monticello Raceway on a Sunday afternoon for the afternoon races.

Stu and I were at the track one night in Yonkers and I remember betting a triple (that's where you pick the order of the first three horses exactly in the order they finish); each ticket cost $3. I was sure the #1 horse was going to win, and the #2 horse and #3 horse were going to come in second and third. I just didn't know which order the #2 horse and #3 horse would come in for second and third place. So, I bought 15 tickets on each combination (1, 2, 3 and 1, 3, 2), which cost $90. Man, that was like a major, major investment at the time. But I was certain I was going to win and not only would I win once but I could win 15 times the payout, because I had 15 tickets on each combination. I was holding those tickets before the race and I was so excited and confident. I gave one of each ticket combination to Stu, so if I won, he won. I watched the race and, unfortunately, I lost. The one horse did win, and the three came in second, but the two came in fourth, not third, so we got nothing. All the tickets were losers.

As we got further along in high school and more into the track, we kept betting more and more and more. And occasionally, we'd win. It still was fun to be with the guys and it was great to yell and scream at the horses and drivers during the race. That was our passion.

Up until I was probably 15 years old, baseball was my passion. I used to walk around with a Yankee hat

(I was a big Yankee fan), collecting baseball autographs and that's all that mattered to me in my life; playing baseball, collecting autographs, and going to Yankee games at Yankee Stadium. Then gambling started to be the thing that mattered to me in my life; it was the thing that started to give me pleasure and fun. In high school, we also started smoking marijuana which just escalated the desire to gamble.

Towards the end of high school, I got into sports betting, but I do want to share one more track story with you before I go there; this shows you how sick it was. I had $600 cash in my closet, I may have been doing some things I wasn't supposed to do to get that money, or I may have saved it up from birthdays; we'll just leave that for history to record.

One night, I took $300 and went to the track. It was probably my senior year of high school and I could drive. (In New York, you could get your learner's permit at 15 and drive at 16.) So, I went to the track, Yonkers Raceway. I was having a losing night, I lost all $300 by about the sixth race. But I was sure that in the ninth race, Frank Popfinger was going to win on a long shot. So, I drove back home, which was 20 minutes, got the other $300 out of my closet, drove back to the track, bet on Frank Popfinger, and lost that race, as well. That was a bad, bad, bad night.

There were many bad nights. Many nights of losing and a couple of nights of winning. My card playing buddies Bob, Mark, and I would share and commiserate with each other. We, Jim, another neighborhood friend, and of course Stu were all big track guys. We had a rotating group of four or five of us who were at the track all the time. And I did love it. Most nights I would just eat rolls and butter at track for dinner to save all my money for betting.

Chapter 4

GROWING PROBLEM

One time during college, my roommate George and I were driving up from Westchester back to Syracuse. We stopped at Monticello Raceway (an upstate New York harness horse track). It was a snowy Sunday afternoon. I went in, handicapped the race from the program, never looked at the odds, bet the #2, #6, and #8 horses in an exacta box. It came in #6, #8 and paid $400. The #6 and #8 were extremely high odds or long shots. We walked out right after the race with a pocket full of money. It was a great day.

George and I spent many nights at Vernon Downs Racetrack while attending Syracuse University in upstate New York. By the way, I did manage to graduate with two degrees. I was a dual major in advertising and sociology, but my real studies were in the art of gambling and drug use, which ended up to be tragically bad career and life choices. So anyway, we'd drive almost an hour to get to Vernon Downs. We actually almost got arrested one night coming back; we were a little high and got pulled over by a cop. We taken to the local police station and were going to get arrested when the cop got a radio call for a robbery. He looked at the other cop and said, 'Just write him a ticket and let him go.' We were so lucky, but it was another bad, bad night.

George and I went to Vernon Downs a lot during our college years. We would go to Joel's Steakhouse for dinner (no longer in business) before the races. George and I would smoke a lot of pot then go and bet. There was no simulcasting back then and of course no online betting. You just bet on the races in front of you. George loved Jack Bailey, a champion driver at the time, and I loved his nemesis, Lloyd Gilmour. I think Jack Bailey won more than Lloyd Gilmour, but we had some pretty good races there. George and I hit big one night on a triple. We won three or four hundred bucks, which was huge at the time. We went out and bought leather jackets the next day and some other clothes. I still have that photo finish picture.

So, there were a lot of nights at the track. I also got into sports gambling very heavily at the end of high school and college. In high school, I bet with a bookie but through one of my buddy's accounts, so I never saw the bookie directly. One week I was down about 1200 bucks at the end of the week. I didn't have the money to pay. I was betting baseball and was in way over my head. I thought I would have to go tell my father if I lost, which would definitely have been a tragedy for me. My life as I knew it would have been over at that point. First of all, the disappointment I would have seen in dad's eyes would have killed me emotionally, then the ramifications for me from a financial and accountability standpoint would have been very dramatic and nothing I wanted to face.

Of course I had no other choice. So, I did what any good gambler would do; I went out and bet double or nothing on a Sunday afternoon game. The New York Mets were playing the Pittsburgh Pirates. John Milner hit a home run for the Pirates, but fortunately for me, Jon Matlock was the Mets pitcher and the Mets won 3 to that day. I won the bet and broke even that week, so I owed the bookie nothing. Then I was back in action! (Jon Matlock is my hero to his day, after all he saved my life!)

Yet, that was probably the worst thing that ever could have happened to me. Had I been stopped in my tracks then and my problem exposed; I may have beaten my gambling addiction at that point. I probably would have been in very good shape and could have saved myself years of pain and aggravation.

Anyway, continuing in college, I was still doing some things I shouldn't have done, so I had access to a lot of money. And I was gambling; I thought I was a genius.

I got much more into sports gambling. I thought, 'Why am I wasting my time with horseracing where I have to pick one out of eight to win? Why don't I bet on baseball and basketball where I have a one out of two chance of winning. Much better odds then horse racing. Right from the start I have a 50-50 chance to win.' I really thought I knew better than most bookmakers and that I was an amazing sports bettor and handicapper of sporting events.

So, whenever I would bet on the Chicago Bulls, the best team in the NBA at the time, I believed that Michael Jordan (the best player in the league at the time) was working for me. I owned Michael Jordan when I bet on the Bulls. I couldn't afford to buy the Bulls; I couldn't be the owner of the team. But each night they played, Michael Jordan was on my payroll. I had some big wins and some very, very big losses, but it was always exciting. Losing sucked but, at that time, just the thrill and action of gambling far outweighed the pain of losing. That would change over time!

Unfortunately, I was incredibly addicted to gambling. I would call up the "sports line" late at night for the late basketball scores. It was a 212-area code, a New York City phone number, and you had to pay every time you called. (Back then they billed your phone bill and I think it was like a dollar or two every time you called.) I would call every ten minutes, probably 10 to 20 times a night as the games progressed. I'd hear, 'This is Vic Cangelosi for the sports line. Ten minutes left in the third quarter; the Lakers lead 201 to 198.' And we would get those ten minute updates that we were hanging on to see if we won or lost. I would stay up till 2:00 in the morning for the late games on the coast; it was not a pretty picture. And yes, a few times I had to intercept the phone bill in my parents' mailbox and pay it before my dad saw it because I wanted to live another day.

Chapter 5

IS IT MY FATHER'S FAULT

I knew I was addicted. I wasn't winning over time; it didn't matter to me. As I got older, after college, I liked to go to the casinos from time to time, especially to Vegas or Lake Tahoe. We didn't get there much. But the great part of gambling in my day, the saving grace of gambling then, was that when the night was over at the track, you went home and you were done; you couldn't gamble anymore. When you went to Vegas, Tahoe or Atlantic City for a weekend, and whether you got your ass kicked or you won, you came home and it was over. When you closed the week out with the sports book, it was over.

There was no 24/7 betting; there was no online gambling. There was no instant access, there was no simulcasting, there was no bet on every play, every pitch, every touchdown, every player's performance. No, it was win or lose, heads or tails, and at least you had a reset; at least you had a chance to get a grip on yourself. The only negative part was the bookies would extend your credit, hoping that you'd lose and you'd get into debt with them.

I had one friend who will go unnamed, who was a very serious gambler like myself in high school, and did very well in the beginning. He thought he was a genius, just like me. He was betting middles and parlays and other bets, and eventually got his ass kicked over a period of time and lost a lot of money to bookies. Instead of killing him, which they threatened to do, they let him pay it off every week for seven years. That's right, seven years of paying weekly. Every week out of his paycheck, he had to give 200 bucks to the bookie. Eventually, seven years later, he paid it off because there was a lot of interest, called "VIG." That was the grossly high amount of interest, usually 5% to 10% per week. That's right, *per week* interest on the money you owed the bookmakers. Keep in mind, these bookmakers were usually associated with some criminal element. But he paid it off and they loved him. What can I say? He was an honorable man.

Just a note: Gamblers Anonymous says you should never pay off a gambler's debts for them because it wipes out the pain instantly. Instead, you should make them pay off the bookie or whoever he owes over time, so he feels it each and every week and remembers how much it sucks to lose and be in debt.

So, as I mentioned, I did some things that I'm not proud of in the height of my gambling addiction. I was not honest in a couple of business deals I was involved with. I'm embarrassed to say what the material we were buying and selling was, so I won't say it, but I was not the most ethical guy. Even back in high school, I took money out of my dad's pocket to go to the track. My dad owned a wholesale paper business; he'd come home with a lot of cash. A lot of singles, 5's, 10's and 20's. It was such a thick wad; I'd take off singles and a few fives and go to the track. I don't know if dad knew or not. If he knew, he wasn't saying. I hope he didn't know, but I kind of got the feeling he did.

In his day as a young man, he, too, was a gambler. He used to run craps games in the streets. He dropped out of college and took over my grandfather's paper business when my grandfather died. In that business he lifted boxes and did manual labor and made deliveries, all by himself running a one-man show. He worked so hard and did this so that he could put his brother and sister (my uncle and my aunt) through college. And he put them through college, and they both went on to have successful professional careers.

He also raised our family very well, making sure we had everything we ever wanted and every opportunity to have better lives. My dad was an awesome guy. He stopped gambling as a young man after he got his butt kicked. (Yes, he did frequently warn me of the dangers of gambling. Of course, genius I was at the time, I did not listen to him). But back in his day, he used to love craps and dice; he was also a big sports gambler. He said there was a heavyweight title fight the same night as one of his college final exams–Jack Dempsey was fighting for the title that night. Of course, Dad went to the fight and missed the final exam, and that was the end of his college career. I knew I had gotten that genetic gambling gene from him. There was no doubt it was in my genes. I don't use that as an excuse; I just say that as a reality.

So, up to that point in college, I was gambling my brains out. I was losing. I was supplementing that through some illegitimate business transactions and I was hooked. I was hooked on every facet of gambling. I was betting on baseball, hockey, basketball. I had a friend who was my connection to his bookmaker so I never dealt directly with the bookmaker at that point and would just settle up with my friend every week. One time he said to me, 'you know, you're betting all these games. 'I'll bet you can't even name one player on the team you're betting on.' It was a college basketball game and he was right. We were just insane and crazy, and it wasn't very pretty.

So, I know the ups and downs, and highs and lows of gambling. I've had the highest of highs, I remember winning $44,000 one night in Lake Tahoe at a craps table, one of the best nights of my life. But I've also had the lowest of lows. I remember losing $150,000 in the stock market on one day in 2008 when AIG and Bear Stearns went out of business and the financial stocks crashed. YES, the stock market is gambling! (It's very convenient and then socially acceptable for an addicted gambler to call it "investing," just as it is convenient for an alcoholic to call them "cocktails.") So, I know what it's like to have big hits, big successes, and big losses. By the way, on that Friday in 2008 when I bought those stocks in AIG, Bear Stearns, and Merrill Lynch, before the market crashed on Monday, I thought I was the smartest man in the world. I was buying these great companies at discount prices and was sure they would rebound the next week. You can call that gambler's intuition… The problem is just like every other gambler; my intuition was wrong the majority of the time.

Chapter 6

HOW MUCH PAIN CAN YOU TAKE

The money wasn't even the worst part of it. The worst part was the fact that it consumed every day of my life; it's all I thought about. After graduating from college, I went to Madison Avenue. I was very high-functioning at work. And although I might be having a conversation with you or having dinner, believe me, my mind was on the game. Who I was going to bet on that night, the next day? Who was going to win? Who was racing? Who was playing? Where could I get some action? And it was just a horrible way to live.

As a former drug addict and gambling addict I can attest it's a good thing when the drugs run out, because even though you may crash, eventually you come back to reality. It's a good thing when you lose all your money at the track or in Vegas or in a poker game with your friends, because at least you could go home and regroup and think about life again.

There is hope and a way out if you want it!

I was about 22 years old and the gambling was just crippling me; I was using drugs, too. So, I turned to my older brother Mike, who I knew I could trust with my life; he was always in my corner and had my back. I called him up one night and I said, 'I have a gambling problem.' And he said, 'No, you don't. You're crazy, you don't have a gambling problem.' I said, 'Yes, I do. And this is the only phone call I'm making. If you don't help me, I'm never getting help for this.' So, being the great older brother he was, he did some research and found a Gamblers Anonymous meeting in Midtown, New York. He walked me to the door of that Gamblers Anonymous meeting one night after work. He asked me if I wanted him to go in with me. I said, 'No, I'm going to go in myself.' I went to GA; I went every week for about a year and a half till I moved down to Florida. That step changed my life dramatically for the better.

In that room, I saw people whose lives had been destroyed by gambling. I got a chance to look ahead into my future and see where it would be if I didn't make some changes. There were some well-known people in that room, all anonymous, who had lost everything. Some had been on magazine covers, yet lost everything to gambling. There were women, housewives, businessmen, bus drivers, retirees… There were young people, old people, black, white, Hispanic; it didn't matter. This gambling addiction cut across every psychographic, geographic, demographic profile you could imagine. We all had the same problem; we were all addicted to gambling.

It didn't matter what form of gambling you were addicted to; horses, sports, casino, cards. Some guy I'll never forget used to go into a bar and play this illegal slot machine that only gave him tickets when he won. Now, of course, he knew the machine was rigged, but he'd sit there for hours upon hours. Stupidly I thought, 'man, does he have a problem.' I looked at him and thought, man, that's the stupidest thing ever. You're playing in a bar for these tickets? I'm so smart I'm betting on Michael Jordan, the greatest basketball player in the world and that night I owned him. And yet, when I looked at his heart and his soul, when I looked around that room, I saw that each and every one of us was in the exact same place. It didn't matter which gambling vehicle we used, and it didn't matter how frequently we gambled, whether it was weekends or once a week or every day, we were all in the same place spiritually broken, bankrupt, defeated, destroyed, and captured. Captured is the word I would use, we were captured like rats in a trap of addiction.

Thankfully, I got to see what the future would look like if I continued gambling. I really was scared straight by what I saw. It wasn't easy to shake that feeling, but it was a realization for me that this was not the path I wanted to go down. I did not want to end up like those guys and girls, and I was so grateful they were there in that room sharing their experiences. Because you realize it's a losing battle, you can't win. You can win for a day, you can win for a week, you can get on a hot streak, but if you continue to gamble, you will lose. The New York newspaper columnist, Jimmy Breslin, a noted sports handicapper and sports columnist in his day said, 'I wouldn't even wish on my worst enemy that he gambled.' That's how bad he thought the addiction and disease of gambling was, how destructive it was. Families torn apart, lives shattered, ruined.

Chapter 7

SOME ARE TRYING TO HELP

Gamblers Anonymous tells us gambling is the act of playing games of chance in order to win money. A gambler is willing to risk losing a sum of money or property in the hopes of winning a larger payout. Gambling comes in many forms, including casino games like craps, slot machines, roulette, blackjack, and poker, as well as horse racing, lottery tickets, sports betting, fantasy football, and even stock market speculation

Gamblers Anonymous (GA) provides a message of hope centered on the idea that while compulsive gambling is a "progressive illness" that cannot be "cured," it can be arrested through a shared program of recovery.

Here are the core beliefs of the Gamblers Anonymous message:

- **The Power of Admission:** The first step is fully conceding to one's innermost self that they are a compulsive gambler and have lost the ability to control it.

- **The Illusion of Control:** GA warns that the great obsession of every gambler is the belief that they will one day control their gambling. A delusion that must be "smashed" to begin recovery.

- **Progressive Nature:** Without intervention, the condition only gets worse over time, potentially leading to prison, insanity, or death.

- **One Day at a Time:** Recovery is focused on the present. Members are encouraged to live the program one day at a time, avoiding the overwhelming stress of solving every problem at once.

They advised their members to follow certain steps. It is a 12-step program encouraging actionable guidance for gamblers.

The Gamblers Anonymous 12-step recovery program like other 12-step recovery programs, such as Alcoholics Anonymous and Narcotics Anonymous, is intended to help addicted gamblers accept responsibility for their behavior and do everything in their power to change it.

Chapter 8

IS EVERYONE WHO BETS AN ADDICT?

Buying lottery tickets every week, betting on a horse race at the track, playing poker with your friends, or wagering on a sports contest does not mean someone is addicted to gambling. Many games of chance are considered fun by a lot of people and can be a thrilling way to dream about winning a lot of money for very little upfront cash. A gambling addiction is born when simple hope crosses the line into intense obsession.

Many gamblers become addicted to gambling because they want large sums of cash really fast, yet others become addicted simply because of the intense rush that comes along with gambling. The latter less concerned about money and more focused on obtaining the thrill or high that comes from gambling. The high gamblers seek is very similar to the high experienced by people who are drug and alcohol addicts.

The fact that a gambling addiction causes people to spend large amounts of money to reach a high is what makes it devastating to so many people. Gamblers have been known to spend everything from their children's entire college funds to every bit of their savings, and more, to fund their habits. Gambling addiction doesn't just affect gamblers lives; it also has a distinctly profound and negative effect on the lives of their families and friends.

Chapter 9

IF YOU HAVEN'T EXPERIENCED IT, YOU PROBABLY CAN'T RELATE TO IT

Ask yourself this, because it is mind-boggling, how could somebody take the family's rent money or mortgage payment, or imagine this, their children's food money and gamble it away? Now, you might say, 'Jack, that's just insanity, come on. I mean, I understand you have a few extra bucks, you want to gamble. Okay, you got into some trouble. But you would never gamble the money your family needs to pay the rent, mortgage, or, God forbid, grocery money, literally taking the food out of your babies mouths so they would starve. Yet the gambler would and, tragically, often does just this.

This is the sickness and disease of gambling; this is addiction. Of course, no one would check that box. 'Hey, I'm going to spend my little baby's food money, so he starves and I'm a bad father or mother.' No one would say that. But yet, this is exactly what can happen to addicts. The addiction takes over their mind, it controls them. These urges are so strong and so devastating. Even though we know what the consequences may be, we certainly can't say we're blind to them, we take that risk, thinking we're going to win this time; this time it'll be different. And just like alcohol, drugs, or any other addiction, gambling is a lie of the devil. This addiction is a sickening, frightening and life-destroying disease.

Chapter 10

THE POISON SPREADS

Well, that was all happening before the internet. That was before online poker came in 1998. So, then came the internet. Unbelievably, so came the explosion of online poker via phone, internet, and computers into college dorms, corporate offices, and into your house and bedroom. I knew that was the beginning of the end. Now with the legalization of sports gambling in multiple states, the epidemic has shifted again dramatically and for the worse. The virus has spread across the country; it has spread across all ages. People are going to lose their lives, their homes, their futures, their hopes, and their dreams. This 24/7 access to gambling is absurd and the damage it will cause is just starting. It is going to get a lot worse as it spreads.

It is impossible to believe that as the coffers and bank accounts of professional sports leagues are getting filled with billions of dollars from online sports gambling, their commissioners, executives, team owners, and even individual states governments, lobbyists, politicians, gambling proponents and corporations (all who are benefiting from all this revenue, as well as the players themselves), do not know the ramifications it would and is bringing.

Gambling addiction has spread nationwide, especially among young men. One study found that once a state legalizes online sports betting, irresponsible gambling increases by 372%. Gambling helplines experience a 75% surge in calls. In New York alone, $22.9 billion in mobile sports bets alone were placed in 2024, generating $206 billion worth of gross gaming revenues and about a billion in net profit to the operators.

The numbers are staggering, but America has sold its soul and its people, and has opened the gates of hell to this gambling addiction. It is unstoppable. Like a drug addiction, it just needs to feed itself more and more until it has destroyed someone financially, spiritually, relationally, and emotionally. People lose their homes, marriages, relationships with their children and family, and their jobs. Their focus, as I know personally, will be on the gambling and the outcome and the next bet, and not the task at hand or providing the love, stability, and devotion a family truly needs.

Chapter 11

THE BEGINING OF THE END

It is horrible. It is mind-boggling; it is soul-shattering and heartbreaking at the same time. What we are doing to our children? We might as well feed them poison. We rally and scream that foreign entities are shipping in fentanyl which is getting mixed in with drugs and people are dying, but we do nothing but applaud as these gambling ads sucker us into betting more and more.

They convince us that if we want to be cool, like athletes and celebrities, we need to have bets on the game because that's how you can be cool. You're either a winner or a loser, and no one wants to be a loser. They offer free bets, free credits, even free money to come and try their thing, just like the drug dealer who offers free drugs to get you hooked and then he has you for life. It is absurd that we are standing by as American citizens letting this happen to our country. We have been brainwashed, bankrupted, bullied, and fooled into believing this is something we need and want.

It's bad enough prostitution was legalized in Las Vegas. So, is that what you want? You want prostitution legalized, too? Prostitutes on every street corner? Ads for prostitution on your kid's Saturday morning cartoons? Television shows normalizing prostitution so that your kid thinks he's missing out if he's not having sex with a prostitute because that's the real way to know true love and satisfy yourself? No, that's not the answer and we know it. At least those of us who know what true love is. Of course, there's prostitution, we understand that. But, it should be in the shadows and dark places of cities, counties, and states in this country, not at the forefront. And the same is true for gambling.

So, what have we done? For the sake of money and obvious pure greed, we have taken integrity out of sports that once claimed to have complete integrity. Baseball, football, basketball, hockey, golf, tennis, NASCAR racing; all these sports previously claimed they would never let gambling anywhere near the sport for fear the integrity of the sport would be ruined or compromised. There were severe penalties or bans for life for anyone associated with the leagues if they bet on the sport. Why? It was obvious we could not have gamblers near professional sports athletes because it leads to illegal collusion, bribes, threats to players or officials, fixing of games, or rigging the outcome so that the gamblers would win, and the integrity of the game would be destroyed.

This is the beginning of the end! And we will find out that players have sold their souls for money? Yes, I know players today are paid a lot of money, but not all of them. Some of them would gladly fix the outcome of the game for some extra cash. Many players today have friends, families, and associates who are pressuring them for a little insight into the locker room. Who's hurt? Who's not feeling well? Who was out partying last night? Maybe you can still win the game but just drop the key pass or miss a key basket. Remember the 1919 Chicago White Sox aptly nicknamed the "Chicago Black Sox" for fixing the world series that year by purposely losing even though they were heavy favorites. Yeah, well now it's going to be an everyday thing!

What about these college kids who don't know if they'll ever make the NBA or the NFL or Major League Baseball? Well, you can bet on college games, too. Many of these kids can certainly be bribed or bought by gamblers looking to make a quick profit. These young kids can ruin their lives literally by selling their souls to the devil.

Chapter 12

THEY'RE OUT TO GET YOU!

So, gambling used to be strictly a no-no. Not allowed, and the integrity of the sport was pure and wholesome, as was promoted and put forth by all the major sports. That has changed quickly in the last decade and even more rapidly since 2020, as greed and love of money took over playing our society, people, and children for suckers became the primary purpose of these major sports books and professional sports leagues. It's all about money! It no longer has anything to do with the purity, integrity, and greatness of the sport. The only time and place left you'll see pure play with integrity and just for the love of the sport is with 8-year-olds on a Little League field who have not been polluted by the world.

Okay, so you have a responsible citizen, 21 years old, who decides to gamble. Now, I understand not everybody is an addicted gambler, but still, this epidemic is ruining our young people. In my day, when we went to junior high school, there was one kid who sold these football sheets and you gave him a buck and you picked winners; he was usually some bookie's kid who was starting early (certainly not a good thing even then), but it was certainly an early introduction into sports gambling. Now our athletes, celebrities and movie stars are telling us to bet on every play or call. The announcers of these games are talking about the gambling line and line shifts and how it affects the betting of the game; it is absurd. They're no longer just commenting on the game. They are hucksters, shills for the gambling industry, bleeding us dry, sucking out our very soul and finances, as we slowly wither away into the gambling abyss, certain to lead to destruction, devastation, and spiritual and financial death.

It is tragic that athletes and celebrities are endorsing this. It's the same as telling your kid to put a heroin needle in his arm, that it's going to be a great high and he's going to love it. It's okay because everybody is doing it.

Chapter 13

SUCKERS

They tell us to play parlays which is the sucker bet of all time, the odds are so against you. Worse yet, they have the announcers and hucksters, many of whom are former athletes who are loved and respected for their on-field accomplishments during their careers, telling you their suggestions on parlays and proposition bets. The websites themselves even suggest prop bets, picking them for you and telling you what the enticing odds are. The reason the odds are so great on your return is because the odds of you winning are so piss poor. They throw proposition bets at you to entice you to make another big sucker bet on individual players and their performance. They make you believe you are a winner, that you will be a winner. The only losers are those who are not gambling and getting in on the action. The truth couldn't be farther from that!

I'm not kidding and this isn't funny. I'm not against gambling; I'm not against recreational gambling. I'm not against marijuana and I'm not against pretty much anything that consenting legal adults want to do, but don't force it on other people. Don't blast it in our faces and don't pollute and corrupt our youth. Don't pollute and corrupt innocent, hardworking men and women who may get sucked into this disaster.

Okay, so now we get back to the explosion of the internet and 24/7 gambling and the destruction of society as we know it. This is a poison, a virus that is going to hurt, kill, and destroy families, futures, relationships, friends, and do a lot of other incredible harm and damage to individuals and society as a whole. It is a tragedy, a national tragedy on the highest scale. America has sold out its families, its children, its future, all for the greed of a lousy buck. It is heartbreaking and the worst is yet to come.

We know the odds of being a major league baseball player or playing in the NFL player, or making an NBA are slim. We also know the odds of being a successful professional gambler are pretty much zero. Perhaps a couple of people can do it over time, but most people will get their butts kicked and lose everything they had. This amazingly disgusting addiction will drain them of their life, their money, their resources, their hope, their future, their passion, their purpose, their joy, their peace, their families, their health, and their wealth, and even possibly their sanity.

Some people may think gambling is exciting and fun, but that wears off very quick. Much like a kidnapper opening up car door and showing you a bag of candy and then trapping you and holding you as a captive that is exactly what gambling addiction is like.

Oh, it's fun at first and you may win in the beginning. But I assure you it is a cruel, devastating disease that will soon have you in its clutches.

Chapter 14

WAKE UP AMERICA...
BEFORE IT'S TO LATE!

Just now people are beginning to realize this might not be a good thing. While it's great to have freedom to do what we want, perhaps too much freedom, especially for our young people, can be very destructive. And yes, it may be. So, what's the answer? If we can't eliminate online gambling completely, and I realize we probably can't, that cat is out of the bag and he isn't going back in, at least not willingly, we need to immediately eliminate in-game per-play, per-pitch gambling. If you want to bet on who's going to win or lose the game, fair enough. And we need to eliminate the hours that people can bet online gambling. Open up a window for four hours a day from 10am to 12 noon and from 6pm to 8pm and let people have at it. This way they will either win or lose based on the games, but not the heroin-like style of each play, each goal, each swing, now available 24 hours a day.

I truly believe I am a great handicapper. My problem is not my handicapping skills; my problem is my gambling addiction! And my money management which

I cannot control because I am an addicted gambler. For a gambler to be successful, you should be able to win at least seven out of ten of his best bet selections (or picks). The problem I have is when I start gambling I can restrict myself to only my best bets for about a week. Within a couple weeks, the train is off the rails and I am no longer betting just my best bets; I have lost control and am betting on everything (all or most of the games not just my *best* bets or picks). Then I get killed. I lose, as do other gamblers because the odds are against us and the more we play the more the odds are against us, and just like any other addiction we can't stop and we can't control it.

The sad fact is that corporate America, the sports leagues themselves, the players included, have sold their souls, bastardized our children and our future, all for the love of a lousy buck, as if these athletes, corporations, leagues, and teams weren't already making enough money off our backs with sky-high ticket prices, concession prices, merchandising, selling of autographs, and just any other way possible to fleece us out of our hard-earned money.

There is no loyalty in sports anymore. Players jump teams immediately for another buck. It is no longer about that; it is about how to get the fan's dollar out of his pocket and into the hands of greedy owners. Now, I am all for the free enterprise system and for people getting paid what markets will bear, but I am not for advertising and actions that will destroy our people's futures, hopes, dreams, and lives.

Chapter 15

YOU CAN'T WIN

You can't win gambling. You can win for a day, you can win for a week you can have a hot streak, but you can't win over time. The house always wins! That's why casino owners are some of the richest people in the world. That's why the state and the federal government, and now the sports leagues, want to be in the gambling business.

That's why the basketball, hockey, football, baseball and other sports leagues are not satisfied with generating amazing revenue in ticket sales, merchandise sales, and TV distribution rights. Now they have to get their hooks in the gambling business. The sports leagues are not satisfied with raising the price of your tickets to $300 or $400 a game so people can't even afford to take their families to see a game without breaking the family budget. They are not satisfied with bleeding us dry; the owners and players greed has become insatiable. Both needing more money at whose expense. Ours! The suckers who buy the tickets, merchandise, and pay to stream the action on TV, and now gamble on the outcome of every hit, pitch, play, and inning.

They turned to legalized gambling to get even more out of us, sucking the money and life out of people, so they can enrich themselves at the cost of our very souls and lives. That stinks so much!

So, sports betting spread from Las Vegas to the Native American casinos to pari-mutual racetracks that have now become casinos. I get why the Native Americans would do it. They are still so pissed off about that $24 dollar deal for Manhattan and it seems they could really not care less if the patrons go broke and their lives are destroyed. Look at the unbelievable and abundant wealth that is flowing to the Native American nations since they have opened casinos here in the United States. They keep building bigger and bigger casinos; look at the Hard Rock casinos in Florida and other states. Their tribal members get paid out yearly to the tune of hundreds of thousands of dollars just for being a member of the tribe, while the Chiefs rake in millions to billions of our hard-earned dollars. Money, that we the suckers keep on gambling with them. The money gets sucked out of the pockets of the American people who are suckered into believing that this is the way to riches and a happy life. I don't begrudge the Native Americans for the fact that they are smart enough to make money off the casinos.

Everyone wants a piece of the pie. Don't we realize we are killing ourselves, our country, our souls, our children, and our families at the same time. What a vicious cycle we have begun of pain, misery, destruction, devastation, and death of the soul of the nation. Remember you heard it here first; this is how it started and this is how it will end!

When state lotteries came everyone knew they were sucker bets, but the states used them to take monies from the people claiming those funds would be used for education and other good things. They told you the lottery makes it better for the schools and education, as money from that would pour into the education system and your local schools via the revenue from lottery ticket sales. What a load of crap that was! How come schoolteachers in so many the states have to spend their own money on supplies because the budget does not allow them what they need?

What the lottery did was give thieving politicians, who are skimming and stealing, more to skim and steal from. More self-dealing, more pork barrel projects that line their pockets, and those of their friends, constituents, and families. And who suffers? Us! You and me. We are the suckers buying tickets and dreaming of hitting the jackpot.

It's a sad joke. All that money people spend trying to hit the big one. And you know what? There are some winners, but it's not you or me, and it most likely never will be! The odds of winning the lottery or about 300 million to one for the big jackpots.

How about fantasy football? Harmless, right? WRONG! It is a devious introduction to gambling, an on-ramp to gambling addiction. It's just another mind-numbing activity luring people away from families, motivation, and the passion for doing great things for the world by numbing themselves while waiting to see if a certain running back ran for a certain number of yards, or a certain receiver caught a certain number of passes, or quarterback threw for a certain number of yards. No more is it about if the team wins or loses or how it did, it's just if this player did good or bad. Wow! This is insanity. Just insanity.

Now for the killer of all time…it is a new website called Kalshi. They call it a 'prediction market' where you can trade on the outcome of real-world events, but it's actually a gambling site where you can bet on almost anything. Ready for this insanity? Here are just some of the ever-changing absurd things you can bet on today on this site. What will the highest temperature in New York City be today? What will gas prices be in the US next month? Who will be the next Fed Chairman? How low will bitcoin go next month? How many times will President Donald Trump visit Mara Lago next month? Who will be the first to leave President Trump's cabinet?

Who will have the album of the year? What will unemployment be in January 2026? How many launches will Space X have this month? Will bitcoin hit 150K? What will Palantir say during their next earnings call? What song will be played at halftime of the Super Bowl? And the list goes on and on… place your bet, mister. It's just entertainment, right?

When I was a teenager in the 1970's, my father owned the paper goods store in Harlem, New York City, where the population was largely African-American. Most of the people in the neighborhood were very, very poor and most of them lived on welfare. And even those that worked were living barely paycheck to paycheck. But, even so, a lot of them played what was then called 'the numbers,' and the numbers were played with the local bookmaker. The winning number would be the last three numbers of the published attendance in the local newspaper at Aqueduct or Belmont racetrack the day before. So, a new number would come out every morning; it was a three-digit number.

These people who were so poor they couldn't even afford the one dollar to play the numbers, but they were so poor that they would play the number each and every day because they needed a way out of the poverty that they were in. They were so desperate that they were willing to risk something they couldn't even afford just for any sliver of hope to get out of the pool of poverty and desperation they were in. And of course, occasionally someone hit that number and won. The payout was $600 if you won. To those poor people in Harlem, that $600 felt like the equivalent of a million-dollar jackpot. But mostly, everybody lost day in day out, just like the lottery. Except of course the bookmakers who continued to get rich.

So, I understand why people who are poor bet and pray for a miracle win. But the addicted gambler is far past that thought process. He (or she) bets out of desperation and out of a full-blown addiction that has overtaken and is ruining his life. He has long ago realized the miracle 'big win' does not exist for him. But in his addiction, he does not avail himself to the opportunities of escape which are available, but instead lives confined in the prison of addiction, his life ruined yet continuing to gamble which has become almost as natural to him as breathing and eating, his life source and a justification for his existence. A true and tragic reality.

Chapter 16

THE END RESULT

This modern day fueling of gambling opportunities has unleashed an epidemic never seen before in our country. An epidemic of poverty, crime, and destruction. You think drug addiction caused a lot of crime, family problems, and problems for our health care system? Just wait. This online gambling is going to finish the job. Our country is going to hell in a handbasket. This is a bad bet and needs to be reversed immediately. We need to put the lives of our children, men and women, families, and country above the greedy desires of corporations and people looking to take our money from our pockets into theirs.

Gambling is a losing bet for everyone. None but a few win over time. The emotional toll that it takes, the relational toll, the financial toll, the spiritual toll, and the toll it takes of the quality of people's lives is mind-boggling and mind-bending.

Now, not everyone is an addicted gambler, and if you haven't experienced it yourself and can just gamble recreationally, I understand why you might not think this is an issue, but also there are also some people who can drive their cars at 120 miles an hour, it doesn't mean they should or that it's safe for others around them. Some can drink alcohol responsibly, and some can use recreational drugs responsibly, but many, once they're exposed to it, become the victims of addiction that is life-ruining and soul-crushing.

This quote says it best: 'Gambling: The sure way of getting nothing for something.

Chapter 17

WHAT SHOULD WE DO? THE SOLUTION

So, here it is. We're giving the wake-up call to America. Some journalists have started to acknowledge the problem, and yet nobody is doing anything about it. When COVID-19 came and we realized there was a problem, we did something about it immediately. This is far more dangerous than COVID-19 for our country, its citizens, and their futures. We need to do something about it. We need to regulate it, control it, and stop the advertising.

You may recall, liquor advertising and cigarette advertising was banned from TV for a period of time, why? Because we knew it polluted young minds, and infiltrated their souls and thoughts and hearts, and we knew the advertising was designed to capture them and bring them into a life of dependency on alcohol and cigarettes. As previously mentioned lets restrict hours people can bet to 4 hours a day (10am to noon, and 4pm to 6pm).

We see the same thing with TikTok and Instagram and Meta. These algorithms are designed to keep our youth on these trails of attention and focus that leads them to destruction and wasting their lives and time. So, now we are trying to regulate this and saying this is too much. Parents are learning that too much screen time is no good. Parents are learning that the algorithms are designed to take their kids down a road of darkness, terror, and horror and some to a suicidal road. We see the bad side of the internet; we see that criminals are using it to lure kids into sex trafficking and to rip people off. We understand this concept, so we want to stop to it. We need to stop this gambling epidemic now.

It has already started; it is already causing destruction throughout our land. We need to stop it now! Immediately! Gambling is a bad bet. As infamous mobster and casino boss Benjamin 'Bugsy' Siegel said, 'We don't have to cheat to win, the house always wins, we just have to keep them gambling.'

Wake up, America. Wake up and save your lives, your children, your families, your streets, your city, your state, and your country before it is too late. We are almost past the point of no return; this is a warning call. Please respond accordingly.

At a Berkshire Hathaway shareholders meeting, Warren Buffett, long recognized as one of the smartest money managers and investors ever, called gambling 'socially revolting,' according to *The Motley Fool.*

'I'm not a prude about it, but to quite an extent, gambling is a tax on ignorance,' he reportedly said, referring to the tax revenue generated by gambling. A government shouldn't make it easy for people to take their Social Security checks and waste them pulling a handle. If you have extra money, don't waste it on gambling'.

If your doctor told you that you had to change your diet or you were going to die very soon I believe you would change your diet. Even though you enjoy the things you were eating, if they were killing you, I believe you would stop in order to continue to have a good healthy life.

The same way if you live in a house with mold, and it was killing you, and the doctor said you need to move out of that house or you will die if you stay there. If the mold in the air is infecting your body and lungs and is killing you, I believe you would move out immediately because you would not want to die. It would be much easier to move out and live a healthier life. So even though you may have to give up something you enjoyed. you would definitely do it in order to live. That is the answer here!

We need to change your perspective on gambling and what it is doing to your life and how it affects you. Once you come to the realization, this is leading me to a place of disaster and I cannot win. It is taking away from me the things I love and not giving me the things I want. Even though it is promising me the things I want, I will turn away from it and put it down.

For many it takes a perspective shift to see the truth to be able to stop gambling, for others they have to hit bottom and lose everything or most things and finally realize the hard way that this isn't working for them. Then they seek help. You can make the decision to stop yourself, or seek help from Gamblers Anonymous, psychologists, therapists, counselors and others who can aid in the treatment of gambling addiction.

My first choice always would be to turn to God, our heavenly father and creator who loves us so much and who does not want us to miss the blessings of joy and peace in this life on earth and in heaven for all eternity. I truly believe if you will give your addiction over to God willingly, He will take it from you.

Regardless of your beliefs about God, make sure you get the help you need, either by yourself or from others and stop this behavior (excessive gambling that is addiction) that will only lead to destruction and devastation.

Chapter 18

I DID MY OWN RESEARCH, JUST LIKE SIGMUND FREUD

I was so desperate to convince myself that the contents of this book were accurate, I had to see for myself what the harmful effect of online gambling could really do to people. While I knew this meant that I would been re-engaging in an addictive habit that I had broken decades ago, I was willing to undertake this experiment to prove the thesis of the book, or my addiction had been lying dormant for decades and was ready to snap back into action. Also, I did wonder if Sigmund Freud really used the cocaine because he wanted to do research or because he wanted an excuse to legitimize his cocaine use.

So, I opened an online betting account on the Hard Rock app and started to gamble on sports. At first very controlled with small amounts of money and I was able to control my betting for a couple weeks, betting only my best picks. I knew what the theory of the winning gambler should be (you must win at least 70% of your best bets). I had some early success doing this and controlling myself, but it didn't take very long, about 3 weeks before I was sucked right back in and betting uncontrollably. So yes, gambling is a progressive disease, just as drug and alcohol addiction. Meaning even if you stop, even for a long period of time, if you pick up and use again or re-engage in that behavior, your addiction will quickly become worse than it was when you last left off. This was definitely the case. I was immediately sucked back in thinking about the games, who would win, and what a great handicapper I was. The ease of betting on my phone and computer and the instant access with the click of the button to be able to transfer money and then more money from my bank and PayPal account into my betting account fueled the addiction even more.

I remember quite a while back, some decades ago, a business partner of mine was a big gambler at the casinos, betting $10,000 a hand on blackjack and losing a couple hundred thousand dollars in one weekend more than once. He said to me when we returned from one of our trips to Vegas, 'with the chips in my hand, when I'm playing with them and betting, it doesn't even feel like it's real money.'

It felt the same way for me with the access to a credit card or bank account linked to the Hard Rock account. You don't see the cash coming out of your hand. It's just numbers on a screen until the reality of it hits when you really have to pay the bill. Believe me IT FEELS VERY REAL THEN.

It frightened me how exciting the in-game line changes were, and how I could bet on a hockey game in the middle of the first, second, or third period. I could bet at any point in the game on any sport and the odds shifted by the minute, by the play. I really thought I could outsmart the algorithm because I knew the teams and their performance and, sometimes I did but many times I did not.

Chapter 19

MY RESEARCH PROVED
MY THEORY

As I previously mentioned, at the end of the day I found myself betting uncontrollably, winning some and losing some. It was no longer about the money because I wasn't tempted to bet more money as I knew this was an experiment, but I was still betting what some would consider a large sum of money. To me, it was manageable. And of course, it is like any other addiction, so I found myself betting all the time and unable to stop. So, in two months I had proved my thesis so I stopped because, of course, I knew where it would lead.

I do want to mention it took me about three weeks from the day I stopped to get back to normal because even though I did stop I was going through withdrawal symptoms. It was impossible not to think of the games and make *mind bets* which is what most gambling addicts do. Even if they're not betting on the game, they pick a side they would've bet on and, in essence, they bet on it in their minds. The experience has the same attention and focus to a game that they did bet on. Then if they lose the mind bet they think, 'good. Now that I got that loss out of my system, I'm ready for a win.' If they win the mind bet they regret the fact that they were not really betting on it. So, these mind bets have to go. Someone once said "I used to be a heavy gambler. But now I just make mental bets that's how I lost my mind."

You also have to completely remove yourself from the gambling world and any thought of it. It took me about three weeks, and I was able to do it. By the way, I would definitely not recommend this to anybody. It was not a fun process. It was a painful process, but I again saw for myself how horrible it really was and how online access increased the intensity of the addiction, the ease of access to it, and accelerated the timeframe in which one got addicted.

Chapter 20

WHAT HAPPENS NEXT

So, what do we do from here?

What happens now? Stay tuned my friends and you will see what happens.

Society will go to hell in a hand basket. Crime will be rapid and out-of-control. Why? Because people, good people, not necessarily criminals, will become desperate as they go into debt and do things they would have never done before. Some may steal, rob, lie, and perhaps even kill to sustain this gruesome habit of gambling.

Of course, the leagues and sports books will make sure they put a 1-800 number on the bottom of their ads for those with a 'gambling problem.' They will use disclaimers with catchy slogans like, 'bet with your head and not over it' and 'admit if you have a gambling problem.' And of course they will state that gambling is for recreational purposes only. Yet, that's like putting some heroin on the table, or cocaine or pot, or Xanax or opioids or meth, or a big bottle of Jack Daniels whiskey or wine and saying, 'hey, you should only have a little bit because a lot will really hurt you' or 'we know there's a lot here but you're smart enough to only have little.' Really? Who can do that? Certainly not me and not most people!

Many people would try to fight off this progressive disease and there are some who can bet reasonably for recreational purposes. But there are many whose lives will be shattered and broken. Many families will be hideously and quickly be destroyed by this dreaded disease.

So, what can we do? We can write this book and tell you this is what's going to happen and it will. It already has.

But just as we saw in Hollywood with good clean television and family values, good clean family fun quickly gave way to disgusting vulgarity and pornography in order to attract more viewers. The same thing is happening now with gambling.

Our nation has turned to crap. Our nation has sold out its children and sold its soul to the devil for a few dollars. And we suckers loved it. We the suckers invited them in. Give us legalized gambling; that's our right! We want to be able to have a little entertainment. What's wrong with a friendly little bet on the game?

Nothing is wrong with a friendly bet. The problem is when that bet becomes an obsession and overtakes your life, and it can happen in rapid-fire succession. You are going to see this thing spread like wildfire as if gasoline was poured all over it and torch was used to ignite its flame.

This is just the beginning. Just watch! There are Wall Street pundits who predict the stock market. Some even predict great stock market crashes and some great stock market gains. My friends, any of their predictions will pale in consequence to the reality and devastating truth of my prediction. Just wait and see.

What would you do if you were driving along the road and you suddenly saw the bridge ahead had been washed out, and you watched as people kept driving over the edge to their deaths, not knowing the bridge was out. What would you do? I don't believe you would pull over to the side of the road, sit in your parked car, and watch as car after car drove over the edge, and everyone in those cars crashed and died. No. I think if you knew the bridge was out, you would get out of your car stand in front of that bridge with your arms waving and screaming fanatically at all who were approaching, 'STOP, STOP. The bridge is out. If you keep going, you're going to crash and die.

So, what are you going to do? Just stand there and watch? Or start screaming, 'STOP! STOP! You're going to crash and die!'

PART II

VIEW FROM THE PRESS BOX

Get the Straight Story from a Non-Biased, Analytical News Reporting Point of View.

BY: JOHN RABE

INTRODUCTION

In October 2025, Americans woke to the breaking news of the FBI arrests of two NBA luminaries in a massive gambling scandal. Active player Terry Rozier of the Miami Heat, and Portland Trail Blazers head coach Chauncey Billups, a basketball Hall of Famer, were taken into federal custody after a long investigation of suspicious gambling activity. Rozier was accused of planning to remove himself from games with feigned "injuries" and sharing the information with gamblers beforehand, who then placed "prop" bets on Rozier's play in those games. Billups, meanwhile, was accused of using his status as an NBA celebrity to lure players into high-stakes, rigged poker games that were backed by several of the major New York organized crime families.

On its own, it would be an interesting and shocking but isolated story. But as any sports fan knows, it's far more likely that the Rozier/Billups story is only the tip of the proverbial iceberg and that the long tentacles of gambling very likely now permeate most of the major sports in America, including at the collegiate level.

American sports history has its fair share of gambling scandals but the ingredients and incentives are now in place to make what was once an occasional temptation into an enormously profitable ongoing enterprise.

Of course, gambling is nothing new. The Bible records Roman soldiers casting lots for the robe of Jesus 2000 years ago. But for most of human history, gambling has been considered a vice, something underground, vaguely shady, and often illegal. For most of the 20th century, if you wanted to gamble legally, you had to travel Las Vegas. In the 1980's, Atlantic City was added to the legal gambling mix. That was basically it.

Needless to say, there was plenty of *illegal* gambling that still went on. From the friendly weekend poker game where a few bucks were exchanged among friends to the large-scale Mafia numbers rackets, gambling has always lurked around the edges of American society.

But over the past decade, America has experienced an absolute revolution when it comes to gambling. The sudden, widespread legalization of gambling, it's normalization in society, and its availability to nearly everyone through the smart phone (including children) has turbocharged the gambling industry and produced frightening effects with no end in sight.

This portion of our book will look at this revolution and how it is changing us as a people and how to rescue our kids from gambling,

Chapter 21

THE LEGALIZATION

Most of us, if we're being honest, have "gambled" at one point or another. Leaving aside more widely legalized forms of gambling like the lottery or playing the ponies at the local track, even those who don't consider themselves gamblers have kicked a few dollars into the office March Madness pool or made a friendly bet with a buddy during an argument about who will win the Super Bowl. All of these were technically illegal in most places but seen by participants and authorities alike as basically harmless diversions. For most people, these were occasional (and usually rare), low-stakes pursuits, and an opportunity to share an experience surrounding a major event.

But in 2018, a culture-changing earthquake took place. The United States Supreme Court issued a ruling in the case of *Murphy v. NCAA*. Up to that point, there was a federal law that prohibited individual states from authorizing sports gambling on their own. But the high court struck down that law (the Professional and Amateur Sports Protection Act) as unconstitutional because they said it violated the rights of the individual states to make such determinations for themselves.

It was a decisive ruling, 7 to 2, which brought together liberal and conservative justices. Often people judge Supreme Court rulings by whether they agree with the outcome and effects of a case, when the Court's job is supposed to be merely to determine if a law or government action accords with the Constitution or not. And from a constitutional standpoint, the Court was largely unified in the Murphy case. They agreed that the federal government could not make the decision on gambling for the 50 individual states. But their ruling did not mandate legalized gambling; it merely allowed the individual states the freedom to authorize sports gambling (or not).

The majority of states (though not all) absolutely leaped at the opportunity offered by the Court. The ruling was issued in May 2018, and by the end of that year, eight states had already legalized sports betting. Dozens more states followed shortly behind, and as of the end of 2025, 39 states plus Washington, D.C. and Puerto Rico had some form of legalized sports gambling.

But the widespread legalization has not come without regrets. Massachusetts, which legalized sports betting in 2022, is now examining significant measures to curtail the industry, including a ban on advertising during televised sporting events. And they're not the only ones.

So, what happened? What went wrong?

Massachusetts state senator John Keenan had an interesting realization, to which he testified before a state committee:

> "When I voted to legalize sports betting, I never thought it would become what it is…We unleashed an industry that now promotes betting on anything and everything imaginable and unimaginable all over the world, 24 hours a day, every single day.

> "I deeply regret my vote, and I want to publicly apologize to those who have lost the opportunity to sit and watch a game just for the enjoyment of the game. I want to apologize to those who find themselves in the dark spaces of betting addiction and to those working through recovery, and to their families and friends. I want to apologize to those who have lost loved ones to suicide because of gambling issues." [1]

Addiction. Financial ruin. Suicide, including among teens. The swath of damage from sports gambling grows wider every day, and the reality has proven to be far bleaker than the rosy picture painted for voters by the gambling industry and its heavily subsidized politicians.

Many people have the attitude, "people are doing it already, so why not just make it legal?" The argument is that it is better to legalize, tax, and regulate the sports gambling business rather than encouraging a black market. (Similar arguments are made for the legalization of cannabis and other drugs.)

But the actual numbers tell a different story. Legalization of sports betting has affected the behavior of millions of people who were not previously gamblers. Widespread legalization is not merely regulating what was already there; it is expanding the ranks of gamblers in America exponentially.

A University of California San Diego study found that in 2017, the amount bet on sports nationally was $4.9 billion. In 2018, the Supreme Court's ruling opened the doors to legalized sports betting in most of the country. By 2025, the total amount wagered on sports in the U.S. was more than $167 billion.[2] That's a *33*-fold increase in just eight years.[3] And in just one year, from 2023 to 2024, the raw amount of money bet jumped nearly 24 percent.[4]

Legalization is an enormous part of the reason for the explosion of sports gambling. But there are other factors that have been crucial ingredients in the mix.

Chapter 22

THE SPREAD OF APPS

Even the mere legalization of sports betting on its own would not be sufficient to account for the overwhelming explosion of the industry since the 2017 Supreme Court decision. Even in the few places where sportsbooks were legal, like Las Vegas, for decades you'd usually have to get on the road and head to a brick-and-mortar casino and walk up to the betting cage with cash (or chips) in hand to place your wager.

But the sudden legalization of sports gambling coincided with one of the most life-changing pieces of technology ever developed: the smart phone. In a world without the internet, bets had to be made in person, or at least over the phone.

When the internet came along in the 1990's, the possibilities opened up, since money could be more easily transferred electronically, and Japan or Poland was as easily accessed as the convenience store next door.

In the late 2000's, Steve Jobs brought us the techno-logical miracle of the smart phone, which allows us to carry the entire internet in our pockets with us wherever we go. Whereas computers used to run programs, the smart phones ran applications, (or "apps") little computer programs built especially for the phone that did everything from helping us pass time in waiting rooms with endless rounds of Angry Birds to steering us, via GPS, to unknown destination on unfamiliar roads.

Then, into this world of smartphones and apps, came the advent of widespread, legalized sports betting. Virtually all the barriers that stood between a gambler and a bet have been eliminated.

You've undoubtedly noticed that it seems like one in every three or four commercials you see on television now are for betting sites and their apps. And the proportion is even higher if you're watching sports.

These companies have spared no costs to line up stars to sell their apps to America. On any given day, you might see Jon Hamm, Jamie Foxx, Post Malone, Kevin Hart, Ben Affleck, or Vince Vaughn hawking one online sportsbook or another, with confusing offers like "Bet $5, get $150 in bonus bets if you win!"

And it's not just actors and comedians getting in on the action. The 2025 Super Bowl telecast featured an advertisement with seven-time Super Bowl champion Tom Brady endorsing BetMGM. LeBron James, arguably the greatest player in NBA history and still an active player, advertises sports betting for DraftKings. The league is okay with it as long as he does not specifically discuss or endorse basketball gambling.

Just a moment ago, we said LeBron James is, "arguably the greatest player in NBA history." If you don't agree with that assessment, DraftKings still has you covered, because the other contender for the Greatest of All-Time title, Michael Jordan, also owns an equity stake in the sportsbook and is a "strategic advisor" to its board of directors.

These gambling companies, through the development and shrewd promotion of their gambling apps, have made sports betting easier and more available than it has ever been. And as we will see later in this book, they have also made gambling through the apps more addictive and more easily accessed by underage gamblers.

Chapter 23

THE COMPLICITY OF
THE SPORTS LEAGUES

Ask any baseball fan to name his or her favorite movie, and the Kevin Costner film *Field of Dreams* will appear at the top of many lists. The movie centers on Costner's troubled relationship with his late father and his father's passion to see the name of "Shoeless Joe" Jackson to be restored to respectability.

Jackson was a start player (in real life) on the 1919 Chicago White Sox baseball team, which lost the World Series that year to the Cincinnati Reds. After an investigation, eight White Sox players including Shoeless Joe, were banished from baseball for life for accepting payments from gamblers to "throw" the Series to the Reds.

The story dominated American headlines and scandalized the nation. To think, a World Series in America's pastime could be fixed! The 1919 White Sox became forever known to history as the "Black Sox" for the stain they put on the game. (And they spawned multiple movies including the aforementioned *Field of Dreams* and the historical drama *Eight Men Out*.)

It took baseball years to recover, and the baseball owners (and Commissioner Kennesaw Mountain Landis) implemented strict rules ensuring that any baseball personnel involved with gambling would be kicked out of the game forever.

The reasoning was simple: if fans cannot trust that the games they are watching are honest competitions, then they will stop paying for tickets. Who wants to watch a sporting event that's been determined ahead of time by gamblers?

It took 70 years for baseball's next enormous gambling scandal to erupt. In 1989, Pete Rose, the manager of the Reds, was discovered to be betting on baseball games. (Rose himself denied the charge for decades against all evidence, before finally admitting it in 2003.)

It would have been bad enough for a manager, who makes all the strategic moves in a game, to be betting and consorting with gamblers. But the situation was magnified by the fact that Pete Rose was one of the greatest players who ever lived. He was a true icon. To this day, Rose holds the Major League Baseball records for total hits, games played, and at-bats, and was a 17-time all-star.

To an entire generation, Pete Rose was the face of baseball. And he spent much of the second half of his life as a pariah to the game, banned for life and barred from the Baseball Hall of Fame that his playing career would've easily earned for him otherwise.

In 1979, two of baseball's greatest-ever players, Willie Mays and Mickey Mantle, both retired from playing, were banned from baseball by commissioner Bowie Kuhn merely for signing contracts to *s*hake hands and greet guests at a couple of major casinos. (Both were eventually reinstated by the next commissioner, Peter Ueberroth.) Baseball saw any connection whatsoever to gambling to be such a direct threat to the game that simply being associated with a legal casino was enough to make MLB swing into action and impose strict penalties. Gambling was viewed as a cancer that could quickly spread and destroy the integrity of the game, which would in turn destroy the public interest in professional baseball.

That's why it might be confusing for a fan in 1989 to somehow be suddenly transported nearly four decades into the future and walk into a Major League Baseball stadium or watch an MLB game on television. He or she would find advertisements for sports betting companies on the outfield walls, the on-deck circle, the billboards behind home plate, the scoreboard, and (in many cases) even in the name of the regional cable network broadcasting their favorite team's games. (Indeed, FanDuel Sports, formerly Bally Sports, one of the largest legal online sports gambling companies, holds the local broadcast and streaming rights to nine different MLB teams, as well as 13 NBA teams and seven NHL teams.)

On Apple TV+'s exclusive Friday night MLB game of the week, viewers are treated to changing percentages on each pitch of the game. The percentage chance of a hit, a strikeout, an RBI, or any number of other in-game events on the very next pitch are displayed on the screen alongside the score and the pitch count. While not explicitly connected to gambling, it's no mystery why suddenly such percentages are in vogue.

ESPN even licensed its own sportsbook, ESPN Bet, until December 2025, when they ended the deal. One would like to think they sensed the problematic nature of combining their status as a rights-holding for nearly every major league with having their name on an "official sportsbook." But no, it was not pangs of conscience that led to the split. It was a failure to capture enough share of the betting market. As ESPN dropped the ESPN Bet deal, they entered a new agreement for a betting partnership with DraftKings as their "Official Sportsbook and Odds Provider." ESPN (and its parent company, The Walt

Disney Company) has enormous broadcast contracts virtually every major sports league and they're all-in on the sports gambling business.

And the ties between sports gambling and the major sports leagues goes much further than mere sponsorships. As CBS Sports' Matt Snyder observed in 2023:

> Beyond the broadcast, some teams are now getting into the gambling action. A sportsbook is currently being built behind the first-base/right-field side of Wrigley Field, home of the Cubs. BetMGM is already set up near the center field entrance at Nationals Park. Caesars (which also has a partnership with CBS Sports) has sportsbooks at the Mets' Citi Field and the D-Backs' Chase Field.[5]

One might wonder why something that was serious enough to result in the banishment of some of the game's greatest players now appears to be conspicuously embraced by the powers that be in MLB.

The answer, not surprisingly, is money. With the widespread legalization of sports gambling nationwide, and the subsequent proliferation of betting apps, an enormous new revenue stream has opened up for sports leagues, which has made it easier for them to overlook their previous concerns about associations with gambling.

While baseball may be the most notable example because of the magnitude of the gambling scandals in its past, they are far from the only sports league with deep ties to sports betting companies. In fact, virtually every major sports league, and every team in every league, has some relationship to the sportsbooks; the NBA, NHL, MLS, WNBA, NASCAR, the English Premier League, and every other professional sports league you can think of.

CNN has reported that the major sports leagues currently make a combined $1 billion per year from the gambling sponsorships. And that number that is expected to drastically climb in coming years, since the amount bet annually in legal sports gambling now far exceeds even the amount spent on lottery tickets, with bettors wagering an estimated $160 billion in 2024 alone.[6]

Plus, the relationships with gambling helps the sports leagues develop and maintain audience share and engagement. Best-selling author Michael Lewis (Moneyball) tells CNN, "It's a way to keep fans engaged in meaningless games. In an era when people's attention spans seem to shrink by the moment… this is like the future of the way that a fan engages with the sport." [7]

With huge amounts of money and a draw for audiences in an ever-more-fragmented entertainment world, the major sports leagues have conveniently dropped their objections against gambling associations. In fact, they've embraced them to the point where gambling is a bigger presence in sports broadcasts than the players themselves. And in the arena, you'll find a sportsbook ad more quickly than you'll find a hotdog vendor.

Chapter 24

THE EFFECTS ON SPORTS

As we mentioned earlier, there is a long, colorful history of gambling scandals in professional sports, from the Black Sox World Series scandal in 1919 through the Tim Donaghy NBA refereeing scandal in 2007. (In that scandal, former NBA ref Donaghy admitted to betting on games that he was refereeing, and giving gamblers inside information on the games.)

Of course, the effect of gambling on the sports themselves is not the most important issue at stake. The most important issue is the effect that widespread, legalized gambling is having on people, which we will deal with in the next chapter. But there is a lot of evidence that gambling is already changing the face of spectator sports, and endangering the integrity of the sporting events that Americans passionately enjoy. And the evidence we have seen to this point is likely only the tip of the iceberg.

Fans can gamble not only on the outcome of games, but on almost everything that happens *within* a game. Through DraftKings, FanDuel, Bet MGM, Fanatics,

Caesar's, bet365, and dozens of other online sportsbooks, gamblers can bet on every pitch, swing, shot, basket, kick, pass, run, or steal that happens in a game.

Beginning decades ago, the rise of fantasy sports began to diminish rooting interest in favorite or hometown teams in favor of the performance of individual players that benefitted one's fantasy team. But that trend away from natural rooting interests has been turbocharged by betting apps and the algorithms that encourage addictive wagering on every event in every game in every sport.

With millions of fans now rooting mainly for their pocketbooks and often risking their paycheck, the passions surrounding the games have reached new and deeply unhealthy levels. "I get death threats all the time, every day," New York Mets relief pitcher Ryne Stanek told the New York Post. "It's not anything that every baseball player doesn't deal with all the time. Like, 'You cost me my parlay; I hope your family dies.'"

From Stanek's standpoint, which he says is just the norm among major league baseball players now, "Gambling in baseball is doing nothing but making the day-to-day lives of players substantially worse. It's just people that recklessly bet their money on just anything that they can and if you mess up their bad life choice, you're the problem and you should die." [8]

Enormous sums are being bet on everything that happens in a game now, and it doesn't take Sherlock Holmes to figure out that these piles of money are going to influence the occasional player, coach, or referee to use their influence on the events to cash in. Even if it's only a tiny percentage, the existence of any trace of gambling activity casts suspicion on all the games.

Professional athletes are, by nature, hyper-competitive. To get to the pinnacle of athletics, athletes have to be driven by the constant desire to improve and to beat the other guy. But that competitiveness which makes people at the very top of their profession great does not always stay within the bounds of the game.

As it happens, I worked with Pete Rose for a few of years at the now-defunct SportsFan Radio Network in the 1990's. Rose was an on-air talk show host on the network, and though he was mainly based in Boca Raton, Florida at the time, he spent a few days each month broadcasting from the network's broadcasting space at the sportsbook of the MGM Grand Hotel in Las Vegas.

If you've never been in a casino sportsbook, it's wall-to-wall television monitors, with every conceivable sport being shown; basketball, football, baseball, soccer, dog racing, and every other sport they can find for you to bet on. Once, after one of the broadcasts from the MGM's sportsbook, John watched Rose bet a mutual coworker on a play in a Monday Night Football game.

"Frank," Pete said, addressing one of the sports update anchors who did regular news-and-score updates during the on-air program, "a hundred bucks says they do an onside kick."

The young anchor, Frank, who was paid practically peanuts like all the other employees of the network who weren't Pete Rose, sheepishly replied, "Um, I don't really make that kind of money, Pete."

No matter. Rose makes a counteroffer. "Okay, if it's not an onside kick, I'll just give you a hundred dollars."

The special team unit came onto the field and executed a regular kickoff. Rose pulled a wad of cash out of his pocket and peeled off a crisp hundred-dollar bill for Frank, who had wagered nothing.

Another time, a couple other staff members and I followed Rose out of the sportsbook to a blackjack table in the main casino, where Rose sat down and proceeded to play blackjack at $1000 a hand. He didn't win a single hand and he lost $12,000 in about ten minutes.

Millions of words have been written about Pete Rose and his gambling issues. But from John's observation, there seemed to be a clear connection between Rose's extremely competitive nature and his gambling. Why would he put $100 on a play where the person he's betting with puts down nothing? Because he needed to have something riding on it to make it more exciting, to give it more "juice." When Rose was no longer able to play the game that he loved (and excelled at), he needed something else to replace the rush of competition and infamously found it in gambling.

The great Michael Jordan was another notorious gambler. While he never endured a basketball-related gambling scandal (though there were whispers surrounding his sudden, temporary retirement from the game at the peak of his playing career), Jordan's legendarily competitive nature led to high-stakes golf games that continue to this day.

When confronted about his golf gambling in an interview once, Jordan denied that he had a gambling problem. Instead, he said, "I have a competition problem, a competitive problem." [9]

Now transpose all of this onto modern sports where gambling is widely legal and easily accessible. It is not difficult to imagine many athletes, who are by nature adrenaline junkies, getting a bit of extra rush out of betting on sporting events including ones that they are directly involved in.

Actually, we don't have to imagine. It's already happening. In November 2025, Cleveland Guardians pitchers Emmanuel Clase and Luis Ortiz were indicted by federal prosecutors on charges of "pitch rigging."

As ESPN (itself a purveyor of sports gambling) reported:

> According to prosecutors, Clase would
> regularly throw balls instead of strikes and
> sliders rather than cutters on the first pitch
> of at-bats in which bettors would wager
> on the individual pitches to be balls or
> under a specific miles per hour threshold.
> The proposition bets, according to the
> indictment, would often be stacked in a
> parlay, leading to greater winnings.[10]

Gamblers won lots of money on these "fixed" pitches, according to prosecutors. Furthermore:

> Clase provided money to bettors to gamble on
> his behalf, texted with bettors during games
> and later was joined in the scheme by Ortiz,
> a right-hander who joined the Guardians in
> a December 2024 trade, the indictment said.

Court documents that became public in February 2026 indicated that Clase may have manipulated pitches in at least 48 different Major League Baseball games.[11]

As a dominant relief pitcher, Clase was in a position to have an enormous effect on game outcomes. This was once the deepest fear of Major League Baseball, which famously hangs a sign in each clubhouse stating the dire penalties for gambling on baseball. But players are receiving, at best, a mixed message when everywhere else they look they see league-sanctioned gambling advertisements and products.

And that was just one among several recent MLB gambling scandals. Just a year earlier, Ippei Mizuhara, the translator and personal assistant to baseball's biggest international star, Shohei Ohtani, was arrested and convicted for using $16 million of Ohtani's money in illegal gambling and bookmaking. Originally, Mizuhara said that Ohtani was paying off his gambling debts for him. But he then changed his story and said he stole the money from Ohtani.

That's obviously a crucial distinction. In the latter scenario, Ohtani is a victim, while in the former scenario, Ohtani, the biggest star in today's game, is making payments to bookies and has direct connections to gambling.

Ohtani has denied all knowledge of Mizuhara's gambling activities, and there has been no evidence presented that shows otherwise. Mizuhara was convicted of stealing the money from Ohtani (among other charges) and sent to prison. But with its twists and changing narratives, the case raised questions in the minds of many, and at the very least raised uncomfortable connections between baseball and gambling.[12]

While the recent MLB scandals have perhaps been the most notorious because of the infamous history involving the Black Sox and Pete Rose, they are far from the only cases of players betting on their sports.

The NBA has had numerous recent betting controversies. We have already noted the headline-making cases of Chauncy Billups and Terry Rozier. Previously, in 2024, the league banned Toronto Raptors center Jontay Porter. As reported by ESPN:

> An NBA investigation found in April that Porter tipped off bettors about his health and then claimed illness to exit at least one game, creating wins for anyone who had bet on him to underperform expectations. Porter also gambled on NBA games in which he didn't play, once betting against his own team, the league said.[13]

These scandals do not merely affect the individual games one of the involved players participates in. They inject a note of doubt into every game.

In the wake of Terry Rozier's indictment, videos began to circulate on social media of Rozier making terrible passes and missing easy shots. Were these plays evidence of Rozier throwing games (or affecting the point spread)? Once the real suspicion of gambling involvement enters the game, it throws everything into doubt. Did the umpire really think that outside pitch was a strike, or is he on the take? Was that kick that bounced off the upright just "one of those things," or is someone helping gamblers with inside connections make money? If fans cannot trust that the competition is on the level, why should they invest their time, money, and passion?

Gambling on sports has occurred just about as long as sports have occurred. But what was once a furtive, underground activity among a few thrill-seekers now completely permeates our culture.

Because of the obvious threat to the viability of the major sports leagues if the integrity of the games comes under serious question, the NFL has reportedly banned certain kinds of proposition bets (known as "prop bets") with its online sportsbook partners.

Prop bets are wagers on specific events within the game that do not directly affect the outcome. Prop bets are enormously popular (and offer the opportunity for making numerous bets within any given game), and include things like the coin toss, the number of yards a quarterback will pass for, how many touchdowns an individual player will score, etc. But in the wake of the 2025 NBA and MLB betting scandals, the NFL reminded its players and league partners that betting is prohibited on props that are:

> …inherently objectionable (i.e. player injuries, fan misconduct), officiating-related (officiating assignments, penalties, etc.), determinable by one person in one play (i.e. a quarterback's first pass attempt to be incomplete) or predetermined (events that could be determined before a game is played).[14]

That final category would include things like whether a player will play or sit out for that game. That specific issue was part of the Jontay Porter sandal in the NBA.

These categories of betting make the most sense to ban, because they are most easily influenced by one bad actor. Players or officials acting in bad faith on behalf of gamblers would generally need to conspire with others to fix the outcome of games, for instance, whose result depends on the actions of numerous people on the field. But any individual referee can call a questionable penalty, a quarterback can throw one ball away, or a forward can miss an easy layup. These were exactly the kinds of prop bets that Clase and Ortiz of the Cleveland Guardians were involved with, purposely throwing bad pitches to help gamblers hit on "prop bets" that an individual pitch would be a ball, or below a certain mph.(miles per hour) threshold.

With the number of betting scandals growing by the year, you would expect the other sports leagues to join the NFL in banning these sorts of bets at the very least. But wherever there is big betting money riding on sporting events, there will be the potential incentive for the participants in the games to benefit by passing along information or altering their on-field work.

These high-profile professional sports scandals have come as a shock to many people. Why would enormously wealthy players risk it all for relatively paltry gambling payouts? (Emmanuel Clase has made $15 million in his career so far with the Cleveland Guardians, and appeared set to earn a contract paying in excess of $20 million per year in 2027.) It seems to make little sense except that everyone loves to be an "insider," and the ability to tell others what you know and give them an "inside scoop" is intoxicating to many. Think of it as a financial form of gossip, which many find irresistible.

But the temptation for college athletes is far stronger. NCAA schools are now able to pay their athletes (something that was verboten for more than a century, but that changed in 2021 with the advent of the "NIL" policy that enabled athletes to earn money from their name, image, and likeness), and top collegiate football and basketball players can now make big money. But the vast majority of athletes still make little enough that a multi-thousand-dollar gambling payout could be very enticing.

Within just days of the NBA and MLB scandals in late 2025, the NCAA announced that six college basketball players from New Orleans, Mississippi Valley and Arizona State were permanently banned over gambling activities. According to the NCAA, "the violations for each case involved betting-related game manipulation and/or student-athletes providing information to known bettors." The NCAA says the violations included fixing games.

In October 2025, ESPN uncovered an investigation taking place.

> Sportsbooks flagged dozens of suspicious bets made by gamblers repeatedly wagering against the same small-conference teams in at least 11 men's college basketball games over six weeks last season...[15]

This investigation overlaps with the New Orleans/ Mississippi Valley State investigation, but also includes more.

> …It is not clear if the syndicate is behind all the suspicious bets flagged in the documents, but the games mentioned involve five of the six schools where the NCAA says 13 former players are under investigation for participating in gambling schemes: Eastern Michigan, Temple, New Orleans, North Carolina A&T, and Mississippi Valley State.

That's 13 players at five schools in five different conferences wrapped up in one dragnet in one year. Does anyone think that's the full extent of gambling's influence on the NCAA?

The normalization of betting also makes it more likely that growing numbers of college athletes (along with college students in general) will get caught up illegal forms of gambling. With millions of people placing legal bets online, an illegal "private" bookmaker here or there hardly stands out. With everyone looking to bet, more than a few enterprising students who recognize that the house always has the advantage have decided to jump in on the house side.

In November 2025, New Jersey authorities charged 14 people in an illegal gambling ring that had ties to college sports and organized crime. According to the charges, an organized crime member directed and financed several college athletes to operating their own on-campus sportsbooks.[16]

These instances of sports betting potentially compromising players, games, and institutions are not decades worth of examples. Most of the scandals we've just sited came out in just one month in late 2025!

So what's more likely? That the authorities have comprehensively ensnared all the purveyors of nefarious gambling activity in sports? Or that the sheer number of instances coming to light just in October/November 2025 means this is just the tip of the iceberg?

Chapter 25

THE EFFECTS ON PEOPLE

1. An Epidemic in Gambling Addiction

Gambling companies come into the states with promises of enormous popularity and tax revenues. Sports betting is sold to voters as fun, exciting, lucrative, and good for the state. What the gambling companies and other advocates conspicuously avoid talking about is the effect that this widespread, legalized, normalized gambling is having wherever it goes. The commercials depict well-dressed people in glitzy surroundings looking at each other's phones and excitedly celebrating their winnings.

But the reality for many, even most, proves to be quite different. The commercials do not depict the broken marriages, financial ruin, addicted teenagers, wrecked educations, and deferred careers that are growing day by day in the wake of widespread legalized betting.

Researchers are only beginning to come to terms with the financial toll from the legalization and normalization of sports gambling on such a widespread level. The great Christian author G.K. Chesterton once wrote:

There exists in such a case a certain institution or law; let us say, for the sake of simplicity, a fence or gate erected across a road. The more modern type of reformer goes gaily up to it and says, "I don't see the use of this; let us clear it away." To which the more intelligent type of reformer will do well to answer: "If you don't see the use of it, I certainly won't let you clear it away. Go away and think. Then, when you can come back and tell me that you do see the use of it, I may allow you to destroy it."

In other words, Chesterton was saying, if you come across a fence, don't just tear it down. Find out why it's there to begin with. Nobody builds a fence for no reason, and once it's gone, you may find out that you needed it.

For centuries, gambling had been widely held to be a harmful vice. It always existed, but it was hidden and kept underground. Even for those who participated, it was considered vaguely illicit. That's how Las Vegas got its nickname: "Sin City." Even until recently, the Las Vegas tourism industry played upon this idea, as in the enormously famous "What Happens in Vegas Stays in Vegas" ad campaign series.

But many, the "modern reformers" who were supposedly going to bring us into a freer and more enlightened age, assumed this widespread prohibition on gambling was just some outdated, puritanical prejudice. So, with promises of fun, excitement, and enormous tax revenues, they swept aside the fences that kept gambling limited. But most never stopped to take an honest, serious look at the question: why were those fences there to begin with?

We are beginning to find out, albeit too late.

A recent research survey showed that one in five Americans now has an account with an online betting service, and 39 percent of American adults bet on sports. Numbers that have been growing year by year. And the survey does not account for the many users under 18 who bet illegally.[17]

And the betting is far from harmless. According to another recent, large-scale study, every dollar spent on sports gambling results in two fewer dollars invested in retirement accounts. A report on the study notes that, "[f]or the 50% of people who struggle to save, the legalization of online sports betting has led to increased bank overdrafts, higher credit card balances and more interest payments." The report adds that "the average household spends between $800 and $1,000 a year on online gambling." [18]

Another set of studies shows that in states where sports betting has been legalized, there has been a decrease in overall credit scores and in increase in public bankruptcies. A UCLA study showed a 28 percent increase in bankruptcies in states that legalized sports betting. Put simply, betting on sports increases the likelihood that you'll go broke.[19] It appears that the effects not only come from betting specific amounts, but from the bad decision-making behaviors that tend to accompany a plunge into the world of easy betting.

Gambling companies don't make billions of dollars by planning an evenly matched game with the gambler. They play on human psychology to get people to keep betting as the hole gets deeper and deeper.

Anyone who has ever had a gambling problem knows about the awful decisions that can follow losses or even wins. "My luck is about to change" sounds like a gambling cliché, but the mindset is a very real phenomenon, known as "the gambler's fallacy." This fallacy says that past outcomes have an effect on future events. While that may be true in many areas of life, it's dangerously false when it comes to gambling. If someone flips a coin 10 times and it comes up heads every time, what are the chances it will come up tails on the eleventh flip? The gambler's fallacy says that tails is "due" making it a good bet. Math says that the chances are 50/50 just like in every other coin flip. Applied to sports, the gambler's fallacy causes a loser to place the next bet because he thinks he's "due."

Often when the losses reach a certain point, the smart decision for the bettor would be to stop digging the hole deeper. But in many, many gamblers, this situation actually triggers an escalation of commitment. Gamblers sometimes call this "chasing losses." The thinking goes: "I have to get back to even, and then I'll stop." But it rarely works out that way. The house has the advantage in every bet.

But the big winner also falls prey to a fallacy that benefits the house: the "hot hand" fallacy. This happens when a gambler thinks he or she is "on a roll." Why would I stop while I'm in the midst of all this winning? Why break a hot streak? Instead, I'll just keep playing until I start losing. But for most gamblers, one loss is not enough to persuade them that the "streak" has ended.

Each of these fallacies--the "hot hand," chasing losses, and the "gambler's fallacy" rely on the same phenomenon; the psychological likelihood that the bettor thinks all of his bets are part of a pattern or a larger trend. The sportsbook's (or casino's) biggest nightmare is the big, one-time winner who takes his winnings and immediately walks away. But fortunately for them, it's not something they almost never see, because gambling triggers the same centers of the brain that other addictions do. An endorphin rush, combined with ignorance about how math and odds work, and with an unhealthy dollop of superstitious thinking thrown into the mix, allows the sports betting industry to thrive while most individual gamblers lose and sometimes lose big.

The sportsbook companies are sophisticated in their use of psychology and technology to rope in bettors and encourage the addictive nature of it. *Scientific American* magazine took a fascinating look at this phenomenon, and how sports gambling has become such an incredible moneymaker with often-devastating consequences.

> Not all forms of gambling carry the same levels of risk. Engaging in a game of poker with friends, for example, is less dangerous than playing a slot machine. Slots have long been casinos' greatest moneymaker because of the machines' incredible pace unlike in a game of poker or blackjack, only seconds pass between placing a bet and winning or losing. This makes the experience more immersive, leading some slot players to enter a trancelike state called "dark flow" in which they become completely absorbed by the game.[20]

Now the gambling companies are using their online betting apps and an ever-growing menu of betting options to essentially simulate the addictive pattern of the casino slot machine. It's a shrewd business model, though one that's not all that good for the consumer.

> Sports betting was once a slow form of gambling, with people mainly betting on the outcome of a game or race in person or with a phone call. With digital apps, people can bet 24/7 and are also now putting money on smaller events, such as which team will score first or whether someone will miss a free throw. And they can string these micro bets together into one big bet called a parlay, a popular feature that has big potential winnings but usually doesn't pay off. [21]

And on top of this, the apps also allow sportsbooks to track each individual user's betting habits in great detail, which allows them to specifically tailor offers, bonuses, and wagering options to get you to keep betting. If you try to walk away, you will likely begin receiving texts offering you a number of "free bets" and other incentives but only for a limited time. It's all designed to bring you in, keep you hooked, dissuade you from quitting, and rope you back in if you walk away.

As Heather Wardle, a policy researcher studying gambling, told *Scientific American*, "Imagine what the tobacco companies would have done if they had known every single time you took a cigarette out of a pack. If they'd have known exactly how much you smoked, when you smoked, how often you smoked, the circumstances around your smoking."

Scientific American cited an audit of ten major sports gambling sites/apps in the U.K., which revealed numerous concerning features, including:

- A sign-up process that is frictionless and often lacks effective age verification

- Deposits or bets with a default amount that is higher than the actual minimum amount, which leads people to choose the higher amount because of a principle called "anchoring"

- Deposits and bets that can be placed with one click

- Safety tools that are hard to find

- A minimum account balance that is required to withdraw money

- Prompts to place another bet that appear immediately after a previous one

- The absence of a feature that displays how much a user is losing during gameplay

- Push notifications and e-mails that stress the urgency and scarcity of betting offers

- Accounts that are hard to close or "immortal" (meaning they can never be fully closed)[22]

(Source: *How 'Dark Patterns' in Sports Betting Apps Keep Users Gambling*, by Allison Parshall, *Scientific American*, January 23, 2025)

All of these features (or lack thereof) are designed to get you signed up and spending money as quickly and easily as possible and then keep you betting and betting and betting. Not unlike the local drug dealer, their entire business model is to get you to try the product, get hooked on it, and then come back over and over again for more.

There is now a flood of studies about the effects of legalized sports gambling. You might hope that states would have wanted to see such studies, or even commission them, before deciding the issue, but no. Most states rushed headlong into the gambling craze, and are only discovering the negative effects in hindsight. And they are growing day by day.

Another university study indicates that, since the legalization of betting, when an NFL team loses unexpectedly there is a 10 percent increase in domestic violence in the team's home market.[23]

U.S. News did a survey of sports gamblers and discovered that one in four had been unable to pay a bill because of their betting. Almost a third of them say they have debts that they attribute to gambling, and more than half of those debts are more than $500.[24]

Anecdotal evidence can be misleading. But in the case of sports gambling, it simply adds depth gravitas to what the statistical evidence already proves.

In an article in The Atlantic in March 2026, journalist McKay Coppins detailed his own experiment with gambling for the 2025 NFL season. Coppins had never gambled, but wanted to do an investigation into how it works in so many American lives. The Atlantic gave him $10,000 to work with.

Coppins described his first bet as "strangely mesmerizing," and said, "For 200 bucks, I had purchased an artificial rooting interest in a game I had no reason to care about. I kept watching even after a weather delay pushed it late into the night, scrolling frenetically next to my sleeping wife in search of angles to exploit with late-game bets."

Finishing his first night of gambling up $20, he dove in headfirst. He began researching strategies, poring over betting lines, and seeking out oddsmakers for tips. It wasn't long before his family accused him of being addicted. Coppins says, "Doing all of this homework heightened my investment in the games. But it also conjured something disconcerting and primal in me." When he'd lost a close bet, Coppins says he found himself viscerally hating the player who made a mistake or failed to come through.

He concludes: "When I'd started this project, I had presented it as journalism; at some point, it had veered into obsession. And as clearly as I could see that now, in the cold comedown from a brutal loss, I didn't know how long that clarity would last. As I scrolled through the apps, my eye was drawn to the March Madness promotions—some of the Final Four odds looked intriguing. On Kalshi, meanwhile, the Oscars futures were calling to me. The temptation to chase would never go away, it seemed. Those fences that I, and the country, had erected—the ones that had convinced me that I wasn't prone to addiction and America that it didn't need to worry about this particular vice after all—suddenly seemed more vital than ever."

By the end of the experiment, Coppins had lost virtually all of the $10,000, and had even put himself on a self-exclusion list to stop himself from being able to gamble in his home state.

Noah Vineberg, a self-confessed gambling addict, says that he's lost over a million dollars in his life. Vineberg is not a wealthy man. He is a public bus driver in Ottawa, Ontario. He wrote compellingly in 2023 in the Canadian magazine, *Mclean's*, that he had quit gambling after years of problem behavior. But that was before a friend pressed him to try out one of the then-new online gambling apps.

At sign up, the app gave him a $2,500 credit. (Offering credits to entice new customers is a common tactic of the gambling companies.) "I figured I was playing with house money sort of" he said. "I only had to pay anything back if my losses took me below $2,500." That happened within about two hours. By the next day, he was already down $500.

Vineberg writes:

> That was my first taste of virtual sports betting, and I was hooked. With a virtual bankroll, it seemed like the money didn't even exist. It was just a number on a website. I didn't have to go to a bank to deposit cash. I didn't need to take out loans. I could just link up my credit card and pay for bets. Most importantly, I could hide everything from [my wife], who works in banking and would

be able to track any other gambling activity. Just like that, I blew three and a half years of abstinence.[25]

Vineberg's bets began to increase, and he found himself $17,500 in the hole. So he did what many gamblers do: he tried to gamble his way out of it, "chasing losses" by betting $17,500 on the Super Bowl to get himself back to even.

He lost.

Now down $35,000, he increased his betting to get out of the hole, while hiding it from his wife (requiring lots of lies). When it all blew up, he went into treatment, which worked until his father died, and he started gambling again as a distraction, and to numb the grief.

> When my inheritance started trickling in from my father's estate, about $90,000 in total, I used some of it to gamble. I also asked my mother for about $25,000, telling her I needed it to cover my kid's hockey fees, replace a car tire. I kept these things a secret from my wife.

If this behavior sounds extreme to you, be thankful. While the amounts of money or scale may differ, the pattern of behavior is familiar to every problem gambler and his or her family. This story, or something much like it, can be recounted thousands, perhaps even millions of times over.

The National Council on Problem Gambling (NCPG) estimates the annual social cost of problem gambling in the United States (which includes things like job losses and gambling-related criminal issues) amounts to about $14 billion. "And this number" notes Felicia Grondin, the executive director of the Council on Compulsive Gambling of New Jersey, "does not account for those who have lost homes, savings and relationships, and are forced to initiate bankruptcy filings."

> The financial damage is only one aspect of the problem. The wreckage in marriages and families is even more devastating, as relationships are torn apart by lies, deception, and broken trust.

As Grondin writes:

> According to the California Council on Problem Gambling, the average problem gambler negatively affects seven people with whom they have close ties. In an effort to recoup losses, they proceed to drain college and retirement accounts and acquire second mortgages, most likely without

their family's knowledge. They hide their addiction due to feelings of failure and do not admit they have a problem until they have hit rock bottom, after the damage has occurred.[26]

The gambling companies brush past this by affixing some small print to their commercials exhorting users to "bet responsibly" and giving contact information for help with a gambling addiction.

But as one anonymous gambling addict writes on Medium:

> "Call 1–800-GAMBLER if you have a problem" is the equivalent of a "Cigarettes cause cancer" sticker on a pack of Marlboros, displayed in the tiniest font at the bottom of a screen as your favorite hosts shill you same game parlays and prop bets on a nationally televised broadcast.[27]

It's hard to take seriously the warnings that come from the very companies whose product that is being sold. But even though it's an inadequate fig leaf the gambling industry uses to cover itself and appear responsible, the number of calls to such gambling hotlines has shot through the roof. A Florida hotline has seen an 88 percent increase in calls. Ohio reported a 277 percent increase in

2023 when sports gambling was legalized there. Virginia saw a 114% increase in its first year of legal sportsbooks.

2. Children Gambling

Data shows that the financial impacts of legalized sports gambling are greatest on young men and even more so on young men in poorer areas. In sports betting zones, young men saw the largest decreases to average credit score and cumulative credit card limit, and the greatest increases in consolidation loans and probability of bankruptcy.[28]

One young writer in a USA Today Op-Ed reported:

> Last spring, when I was a senior in high school, I noticed a friend furiously tapping his phone during class. He wasn't texting with a friend. Instead, he was placing a bet of well over $100. He was a teenager secretly using his mom's credit card. He's not alone. At my school, kids of all grades were diving into the world of online sports betting, some spiraling into debts that could wreck their lives.[29]

He adds:

> The fallout is more than financial. It can lead to a son having to explain to his mother

why money is missing. Or to a teenager withdrawing from his friends out of shame and embarrassment. Schoolwork can suffer while students chase their losses with more bets.

Now with football, some of my peers don't feel like watching an NFL game is exciting anymore without money on the line. That's what makes this season dangerous: Every game is a gambling opportunity.

There are stories for days like this. The problem of adolescent gambling may be far worse than anyone had imagined. A recent survey of over 2200 people between the ages of 14 and 21 recently revealed that 68 percent had gambled over the previous year, with 11 percent gambling more than twice a week.[30] A larger Canadian study of 38,000 youth showed that nearly two-thirds of 12-18 year-olds had gambled in the past year.[31]

The New York Council on Problem Gambling did a survey of students that found even grimmer results. Their survey showed that 90 percent of high school students had gambled at least once over the past year.

One of them, a 17-year-old high schooler named Max, was introduced to readers by the New York Post:

He estimates 80% of the boys in his class have placed a bet and probably 40% gamble regularly using their parents' accounts.

Max's dad opened a FanDuel account using his own Social Security number, date of birth and banking info. Verification required by the major betting apps and then turned it over to the 17-year-old.

"We'd be saying, 'Oh, yeah, it's not a big deal,'" Max recalled of how he and his friends talked their parents into creating accounts for them. "'You know, we all have it, and we're not betting a lot of money.'"

"I said fine. I just didn't think anything about it. It was something that he and his friends were all doing," Max's dad, who works in finance, admitted to The Post.[32]

Teen boys tend to have higher propensity towards impulsive behavior and lower ability to manage it than their female counterparts, which makes them ideal customers for the online sportsbooks. Dr. Marc Potenza, the director of Yale University's Center of Excellence in Gambling Research, says that teenagers are particularly susceptible to gambling, and that a possible reason is that different parts of the brain develop at different rates, and in teenage boys (who are most susceptible), the prefrontal cortex which regulates impulsivity and decision-making is slow to develop.[33]

The sportsbooks ensure that the bets are only placed by people of legal age--in theory. But according to most observers, the safeguards are easily skirted by a motivated young gambler. And the young gamblers are motivated, with sports gambling offering fixes of excitement that are hard to replicate elsewhere. Once again, this is by design.

The American Psychological Association's *Monitor on Psychology* magazine took an in-depth look at the effects of gambling on the brain and vice-versa, and who is most vulnerable to gambling addiction. They noted the especially addictive properties of sports betting for younger people:

> Compared with other kinds of gambling, the in-game betting offered during sports games is highly dependent on impulsivity, Dr. Lia Nower, director of the Center for Gambling Studies at Rutgers University said. There are opportunities to place bets during the game on everything from who will win the coin toss to which quarterback will throw 100 yards first to how long the national anthem will last. And impulsivity is

particularly common in younger people and among sports fans caught up in the emotion of a game, Nower said.[34]

Is your kid gambling? Most parents don't think so, including the parents of kids who are gambling behind their parents' backs. But it can be crucial to their future and their well-being for parents to discover it and nip it in the bud.

Richard Anemone, a licensed as a mental health counselor in New York State, has some vital advice for parents. Look for the warning signs and be proactive in addressing them. Anemone writes:

> Adolescents may access gambling through online platforms, fake IDs, or by participating in informal or underground gambling activities. To address adolescent gambling, parents, educators, and communities need to take proactive steps to educate adolescents about the risks of gambling, monitor online activities, implement parental controls on devices, limit access to funds, be a role model, encourage healthy hobbies, and encourage open communication about finan-ces and decision-making.

A hands-off approach on the part of parents has led to social media addiction and it's now helping exacerbate gambling addiction as well. Parents probably should not hand their kids credit cards (that they don't keep an eye on) and unfettered screen access. And mindful parents should also keep any eye on their kids' moods and behaviors (though this is good advice even when gambling is not an issue). Anemone says:

> Warning signs of adolescent gambling may include sudden shifts in behavior, such as increased secrecy, mood swings, irritability, or withdrawal from family and friends. A noticeable decline in academic performance, missed assignments, or a lack of interest in previously enjoyed activities. Unexplained money problems, frequent borrowing, or stealing to fund gambling activities. Constantly talking about or being preoccupied with gambling-related topics, even if it's just casually discussing odds or strategies. Changes in social or a shift in friendships, particularly if the new friends are involved in gambling activities. Items of value going missing, potentially sold or pawned to finance gambling. Engaging in deceptive behavior, such as lying about the extent of gambling involvement or hiding

losses. Increased levels of stress, anxiety, or depression may be linked to gambling activities. Persistent attempts to recover losses through continued gambling, leading to a cycle of escalating bets. Neglecting responsibilities at home, school, or work due to a focus on gambling.[35]

Treatment to break the pattern is important. Many parents, when they discover their child has gotten into gambling trouble, bail him or her out by paying off their debt. But most experts say that merely enables the gambling behavior.

"Every person addicted to gambling says, 'If I hit the jackpot today, I make back all of the money that I lost over the last decade, and none of the harm is here,'" former gambling addict Sam DeMello tells USA Today. "To get somebody into abstinence, you have to kill that fantasy," he advises.[36]

And it can be a matter of life and death. According to the American Psychiatric Association, one in five people with a gambling disorder will attempt suicide. About one half will at least think about suicide. The APA notes that, "gambling disorder has been shown to carry the highest suicide risk out of any other substance use or addictive disorder." [37]

Ted Koppel, the legendary television news reporter, recently sounded the alarm on CBS News. The dangers of sports gambling are becoming more widely known… although well after most states rushed into legalizing it.

Koppel interviewed gambling therapist Harry Levant, who had his own breaking point when he hit rock bottom with a gambling addiction. Levant now treats other gambling addicts.

Koppel reports:

> Levant learned his lessons the hard way. He's a recovering gambling addict. "Gambling addiction took my mind, my soul, body, and conscience," he told Congress.
>
> Levant is a disbarred lawyer, who had been stealing from his clients to cover his gambling debts. He caught a break with a sympathetic judge who – recognizing his addiction – placed him on probation for eight years, ordered him to continue treatment, and told Levant, "This doesn't have to be the end. You can do something with this one day."

Three gambling addicts being treated by Levant-- Andrew, Shaun, and Brian--sat down for interviews with Koppel.

"I know a lot of people that are under the age of 18," said Andrew. "They're 16, 15, and they're openly in school talking about all the wagers they got."

They use personal information from parents or an older sibling. "Usually it's a Social Security number," said Andrew. "It might be a driver's license. And then they're taking on that identity."

....And gambling addiction at any age, as Shaun recalls, can be devastating. At one point he was reduced to sleeping in his car. "When I was in the teeth of it, it's all that mattered. My marriage didn't matter. My job didn't matter. My daughters didn't matter. Gambling was the only thing that mattered," he said.

One of the recovering addicts told Koppel that his gambling, which was so addictive that he was taking his phone into the shower with him in order to keep placing bets, led him to the end of his rope.

Andrew said he had considered suicide: "Yes, sir. I … I was gonna give it a shot. I was calm about it. I accepted it. I wanted to do it. I personally had a letter written out. So, yes, it was gonna happen. And thankfully, my dad called the authorities up here, and just before I could end my life, I got a knock on the door." [38]

So what should parents be on the lookout for in their kids? Whether it's you, your spouse, or your child, it's important to know the signs of a gambling addiction.

SIGNS OF GAMBLING ADDICTION

According to the American Psychiatric Association, signs of a gambling addiction can include:

- Frequent thoughts about gambling.

- Need to gamble with increasing amounts to achieve the desired excitement.

- Repeated unsuccessful efforts to control, cut back on or stop gambling.

- Restlessness or irritability when trying to cut down or stop gambling.

- Gambling when trying to escape from problems or negative mood or stress.

- After losing an item of value by gambling, feeling the need to continue to get even.

- Often gambling when feeling distressed.

- After losing money gambling, often returning to get even.

- Lying to hide the extent of gambling involvement.

- Losing important opportunities such as a job or school achievements or close relationships due to gambling.

- Relying on others to help with money problems caused by gambling.

According to the ASA, the presence of four or more of these signs can lead to a formal diagnosis of gambling addiction. But for younger people, especially boys, trouble can begin before there is grounds for a formal diagnosis of "addiction."

The brain (especially the prefrontal cortex) is still being formed in young men, and the dopamine rush of instant and easily-accessible gambling can affect the development of the brain. By the time an addiction is discovered, it's too late to prevent it. At that point, it can only be treated, but as with most addictions, recovery is a difficult process with high rates of relapse, because the pleasure centers of the brain become so closely connected to the gambling behavior.

And a gambling addiction presents problems beyond those even found in alcohol and drug abuse. "Gambling, unlike any other addiction, is associated with cognitive distortions," says Dr. Timothy W. Fong, clinical professor of Psychiatry at UCLA. "People say, 'If I keep gambling then eventually I'll win.' You don't say that about alcohol, tobacco or cocaine." [38] And like with many other addictions, the user begins to see the problem itself as the solution to the problem. One more bet, one more drink, one more hit will make things better.

American has hardly begun to grapple with what is happening to the next generation of kids, who are growing up in a world where sports gambling is incessantly advertised on TV, the web, and at actual sporting events. Where the apps are endorsed by major pop culture figures. Where gambling has been taken out of the shadows and made a normal feature of daily American life. Where the different kinds of bets that can be placed have multiplied exponentially. Where the process of placing bets is as easy as tapping your phone screen. Where the restrictions set up to keep the kids from gambling before they're of legal age are flimsy at best and purposely evadable at worst. Not only are we turning them into gambling addicts, we're letting them have their minds altered. We're almost encouraging them to mess up their brain chemistry (which the dopamine hits provided by addictive social media have already laid the tracks for). We have set the next generation of young people up for disaster, especially young men.

We have never allowed commercials promoting crack or heroin, let alone a flood of messages making it seem appealing. But many kids are having their educations derailed and their professional futures diverted, not to mention falling into deep financial straits and lifelong addiction issues, as a result of something that the entire culture tells them is fun, exciting, harmless, and even glamorous.

Legalized, normalized sports gambling has indeed turned out to be a bad bet.

Chapter 26

SOLUTIONS

Unfortunately, there are not many easy solutions to be found. But most experts can agree on a few keys.

It is very unlikely that sports gambling will be made illegal again, at least not at a national level. There is too much money at stake for the states, for the influential sports team owners who fund political campaigns, for the networks that rake in the ad dollars, and for the millions who now play on a daily basis. The constitutional issues seem settled (at least under the current composition of the Supreme Court), so a federal ban is not likely to return anytime soon. Legalized sports gambling is not a genie that can easily be put back into the proverbial bottle.

As with so many other social pathologies, the biggest key is active parental involvement. As any parent knows, this has to start young. Suddenly imposing a new regime of seemingly stricter rules is not likely to succeed with a 15-year-old. But building in patterns of accountability, oversight, and communication early can smooth the way for things like limits on screen time and monitoring our children's app usage.

Among spouses, open communication and account-ability are also key. Small changes in mood should be put on the table and talked about; not to mention huge changes, like secret bank accounts, sudden unexplained changes in account balances and credit ratings, or a sudden proliferation of credit cards.

Beyond the family, voters should begin to demand bans or severe restrictions on sports gambling advertising. Until the mid-1990's, distillers of hard liquor voluntarily agreed not to advertise on television where children were likely to see it, instead more carefully targeting their ads to those over legal drinking age through print and other media. Even in 2026 America, you still cannot show someone drinking whiskey--in a commercial for whiskey!

Yet you can show singer Post Malone staring at his phone and pumping his fist at his latest gambling win. A study of the 2025 NHL Stanley Cup telecast revealed that viewers saw gambling ads or logos once every 13 seconds! [40] The absolute inundation of audiences, including kids, with gambling ads is irresponsible at best. If laws don't change, consumer pressure on the broadcasters can make an impact.

Such bans will be difficult to enact, especially considering the 2018 Supreme Court decisions. But lawmakers have already proposed a federal ban on sportsbook advertising during actual sporting events, and between 8am and 10pm when children and teens are most likely to be watching. But voters and taxpayers have the ability to urge lawmakers on a local and state level (who are closer to them and usually more responsive) to get something done.

CLOSING THOUGHTS

Okay there you have it. Our thoughts, insights, and opinions on what is going on with the onslaught of online gambling and the way it is bombarding not only our youth, but all hard-working Americans. Online gambling and its 24/7 access is challenging the narrative of what is appropriate and acceptable behavior and where it is leading. We believe it leads to life-changing, damaging, heartbreaking, and devastating results for individuals, families, and our country.

We hope you take this to heart. We hope if you or someone you know is struggling with gambling addiction, they would get help immediately! Gamblers Anonymous is a wonderful program that can help people overcome gambling addiction. Also, if you're a person of faith, we would certainly suggest that you pray to God to take this addiction or urge away from you. There are also counselors and psychologists who can help people overcome gambling addiction.

One thing for sure, gambling is a sucker's bet. And when you engage in it, become enthralled with it, and are addicted to it, you are gambling with your life!

Hopefully, it is not too late. The saying goes, 'you don't have to wait till the elevator hits bottom to hit the stop button and get off.' It is far better to deal with this problem now, at an earlier stage in your life than to suffer for another 10, 20, 30, 40, or even 50 years as a prisoner of the horrible addiction of gambling.

This is the one bet you can automatically win by never making. What you win back is your joy, your peace, your focus on life, your relationships, your purpose, passion, goals, dreams, hopes, and futures.

You win back your self-respect and dignity that addiction stole from you. You win back your integrity, your sense of self-worth, and the knowledge and satisfaction that you did not let this addiction drag you into the pit of despair, into financial, spiritual, emotional, and physical ruin. You can escape from the pit of hell. You can escape the devastation of your mind, soul, spirit, and basically your life from going down the drain. You deserve a life free from this life sucking addiction.

We wish you all of life's best blessings. There is a battle going on. You have to pick which side you're on, then fight and have victory. Please choose the right side of this. You are betting your life on it.

Jack and John

SPECIAL THANKS

Very special thanks to four people who have worked with me over the years to continue to make my books the best they can possibly be and are an integral part of the process. I am so grateful for their support and appreciation.

John Rabe. Who co-authored this book with me and has been involved in so many of my books since 2010. Thank you John for your unending support. I am so glad we finally got to write one together. Your contributions are invaluable. I pray, as you do, this book would impact many and help save lives from the throes of a destructive addiction. Your insight, mindset and super intelligent and analytical mode of thinking is an inspiration to me!

Elizabeth Levine. My amazing wife. Thank you so much for your undying loyalty and for your time and effort you put into this book and so many of my other projects. Most importantly your love and support has encouraged me through the years and inspired me. You're an amazing editor and I so much appreciate your suggestions, comments and keeping the facts straight and helping me to not sound like an idiot... Although I do realize sometimes that's impossible...smile! I love you and appreciate you and am truly blessed to have you as my wife and friend.

Scott Wolf. Thanks Scott for your amazing design and layout creativity and your creative expertise. AI will never replace you! You are awesome and I so much appreciate you being at the ready to bring a new project to the market and help me get it to completion. Your ability to think out-of-the-box and to create design and layout, whether it's my books or many other projects for myself or others is a unique and true talent and gift. I'm blessed to have you as a friend and to be able to work with you.

Scott Brown. Thanks for the quick turnaround and review of the book draft. I know you had short notice on this one buddy, but as usual you came to the rescue. Your insight was invaluable and your comments helped me organize my thoughts and put me on the right track I needed to be able to finish this book in a timely and orderly manner. So thanks again. Your new nickname is no longer Scott "Downtown" Brown but now Scott "Superman" Brown.

Thank you all. Keep the train rolling!

To God be the glory.

Jack

REFERENCES

1. https://www.legalsportsreport.com/246462/massachusetts-senator-apologizes-for-yes-vote-on-sports-betting/

2. https://www.espn.com/espn/betting/story/_/id/48045855/sports-betting-hits-record-1696-billion-revenue-2025

3. https://today.ucsd.edu/story/study-reveals-surge-in-gambling-addiction-following-legalization-of-sports-betting

4. https://sports-entertainment.brooklaw.edu/sports/from-marlboros-to-moneylines-why-sports-gambling-ads-may-need-a-regulatory-check/

5. https://www.cbssports.com/mlb/news/how-mlb-is-trying-to-embrace-legalized-gambling-without-ostracizing-fans-or-risking-its-integrity/

6. https://www.cnn.com/2025/10/25/business/this-is-how-sports-gaming-has-become-crucial-to-leagues-bottom-lines

7. Ibid.

8. https://nypost.com/2025/11/07/sports/new-york-stars-bombarded-with-social-media-hate/

9. https://bleacherreport.com/articles/2890029-michael-jordan-on-gambling-hobby-i-have-a-competition-problem

10. https://www.espn.com/mlb/story/_/id/46906636/guardians-emmanuel-clase-luis-ortiz-indicted-pitch-rigging

11. https://www.espn.com/mlb/story/_/id/47842376/guardians-clase-allegedly-rigged-pitches-48-games-document-says

12. https://www.cbssports.com/mlb/news/shohei-ohtani-gambling-scandal-explained-everything-we-know-as-ippei-mizuhara-pleads-guilty-to-bank-fraud/

13. https://www.espn.com/nba/story/_/id/40490035/banned-nba-player-jontay-porter-charged-felony

14. https://www.espn.com/nfl/story/_/id/46957763/in-memo-nfl-details-efforts-curb-prop-betting-light-wider-gambling-probes

15. https://www.espn.com/mens-college-basketball/story/_/id/46607545/records-gambling-syndicate-ncaa-basketball-suspicious-bets

16. https://www.espn.com/college-sports/story/_/id/46957471/14-arrested-mafia-backed-betting-ring-involving-athletes

17. https://www.sbu.edu/news/news-items/2024/02/05/st.-bonaventure-siena-research-survey-reveals-almost-1-in-5-americans-have-an-online-sports-betting-account

18. https://www.kmbc.com/article/kansas-study-online-sports-betting-costs-americans-retirement/62037985

19. https://www.nbcnews.com/business/consumer/online-sports-gambling-bankrupting-households-reducing-savings-rcna167235

20. https://www.scientificamerican.com/article/how-sports-betting-apps-use-psychology-to-keep-users-gambling/

21. Ibid.

22. Ibid.

23. https://www.opb.org/article/2024/10/30/think-out-loud-university-of-oregon-sports-gambling-intimate-partner-violence-football/

24. https://www.usnews.com/banking/articles/2025-sports-betting-and-debt-survey

25. https://macleans.ca/society/addiction-sports-betting-gambling/

26. https://www.theguardian.com/us-news/article/2024/sep/05/gambling-us-policymakers-prevention-treatment

27. https://packripewing.medium.com/sports-gambling-is-truly-bad-945ec-723baf9

28. https://aibm.org/research/how-sports-betting-can-harm-young-men/

29. https://www.usatoday.com/story/opinion/voices/2025/09/20/sports-betting-gambling-apps-nfl-gen-z/85991876007/

30. https://redwoodbark.org/91272/sports/uncovering-the-epidemic-of-youth-sports-gambling/

31. https://www.apa.org/monitor/2023/07/how-gambling-affects-the-brain

32. https://nypost.com/2025/10/16/lifestyle/sports-betting-addiction-on-the-rise-with-teens-according-to-kids/

33. https://www.apa.org/monitor/2023/07/how-gambling-affects-the-brain

34. https://www.apa.org/monitor/2023/07/how-gambling-affects-the-brain

35. https://behavioralhealthnews.org/adolescent-gambling-a-growing-concern/

36. https://www.usatoday.com/story/life/health-wellness/2025/05/13/sports-betting-college-kids-teens-health/83391628007/

37. https://www.psychiatry.org/patients-families/gambling-disorder/what-is-gambling-disorder

38. https://www.cbsnews.com/news/online-betting-the-dangers-of-sports-gambling-addiction/

39. https://www.uclahealth.org/news/article/gambling-addiction-can-cause-psychological-physiological-health-challenges

40. https://bircheshealth.com/resources/gambling-logos-ads-us-sports